Modern-Day Etiquette fc

MASTER THE ART OF MANNERS

Dr. Clinton Lee

Executive Director of the Asia Pacific Wine and Spirit Institute

PAGE STREET
PUBLISHING CO.

PAGE STREET
PUBLISHING CO.

First published in 2023 by
Page Street Publishing Co.
27 Congress Street, Suite 1511
Salem, MA 01970
www.pagestreetpublishing.com

Distributed by Macmillan, sales in Canada by The Canadian Manda Group.

27   26   25   24   23   1   2   3   4   5

ISBN-13: 978-1-64567-917-2
ISBN-10: 1-64567-917-9

Library of Congress Control Number: 2022949981

Cover and book design by Emma Hardy for Page Street Publishing Co.
Cover and author photos by James Stockhorst

Printed and bound in the United States

Dedication

I would like to dedicate this book to my dearest parents and all the extraordinary teachers that I have had the privilege of knowing in my life. I thank them all for their wisdom, encouragement, and their life-long gift to me, the insatiable desire of seeking new knowledge daily.

CONTENTS

FOREWORD

DR. CLINTON LEE and I have been close friends since we met in Africa in 1986. Over the intervening years, he has earned a range of professional credentials, including degrees in accounting, an MBA in finance, and a doctorate in business. Being the polymath that I know him to be, he added several wine and spirit certifications like the Asia Pacific Wine and Spirit global certification; Wine & Spirit Education Trust certified educator; international sherry educator; sake, whiskey, and cigar credentials; and many more, too numerous to mention.

He has worked all over the world, starting a broad range of new business ventures—all successful. His remarkable success has been possible due, in large part, to his ability to empathize and to learn the customs, values, and etiquette of different cultures and business environments, and in turn building trust and personal relationships.

He has learned to be sensitive to his environment and to avoid culture-bound "mistakes" that can undermine or destroy trust and respect. These are key practical skills and relate to communication in every environment, including one's home community and profession. He summarizes these skills with the term "etiquette." A violation of the etiquette can torpedo a meeting, a relationship, or a business opportunity. These violations are generally not intentional and sometimes not even consciously observed, even by the offended parties; yet, they are deadly.

Of greatest importance, this book is not an inventory of "tricks" to masquerade as someone you are not. Rather, the act of empathizing with and assimilating to other customs and values is transformative. It is very satisfying. Also, cumulative. Success in learning the etiquette of one culture makes it easier to master the next. It is like a muscle that is strengthened as it is used.

This book provides a path for you to develop the skills and confidence to be respected and effective in the full range of interactions that constitute the core of your personal and professional relationships.

—Dr. Victor Levine, PhD

INTRODUCTION

IF YOU ARE READING THIS BOOK, there are several reasons why you might have an interest in etiquette. Perhaps you are hearing the word etiquette being used more frequently and increasingly in the media, and it has ignited your curiosity. Possibly, there is a genuine and keen desire to learn about etiquette, how it pertains to you, and how it may positively help you seamlessly navigate social circles and successfully interact with the business world. Or maybe you were recently embarrassed in a social situation, and this has left your personal flag of self-esteem tattered and torn, fluttering furiously and carelessly in the winds of the unfamiliar social landscape. Whatever the reason, continue reading this book to increase your self-confidence, uplift your social awareness, gain the respect of other cultures through your thoughtful behavior, and be admired for your global, balanced, and measured business approach.

Throughout this book, you will learn a great deal about manners, which are defined as the socially accepted ways we behave toward other people. But to properly show respect for the customs, traditions, values, and feelings of others—to truly have proper manners—you must first become a master of etiquette.

According to the Cambridge dictionary, etiquette is defined as "the set of rules or customs that control accepted behaviour in particular social groups or social situations." To become a master of these rules for your own community or culture is one thing, but to truly master the art of manners, you must open yourself to learning the rules and customs of others in the world.

Clearly, etiquette and manners differ and constantly evolve according to the traditions and customs valued by each country and generation. What is the norm in one country can be entirely the opposite in another. With this book and your hunger to learn, you are ready to take a journey through the evolution and variations of present-day etiquette with me. Let's continue this adventure together and discover the power of etiquette.

Etiquette is very near and dear to me, as it has molded me in various shapes, styles, and forms over the years, helping me adapt to whichever situation I find myself in. The world of travel is my never-ending university of life where I learn, listen, and observe the etiquette of different cultures.

As a young boy growing up in Southern Africa, where apartheid was responsible for segregating all aspects of society, I had to understand the different components of each segment within that society, including their norms and behavior, to navigate through them smoothly. In addition to recognizing those rules and customs, I also needed to learn the cultural expectations of my home and school. When you add to my personal life recipe my immigrant parents with a Chinese and Mozambique heritage and a Jesuit education, you can see how my life was quite flavorful from the start. My education, although stern, opened the world of classical European knowledge and etiquette for me, instilling in me a great appreciation for the acquisition of knowledge. I gleefully blame this residual influence for my insatiable desire to learn.

At home, there was a strong Asian influence in all aspects—language, food, and customs. There was also this gray area between home and the segregated world, which allowed me during my formative years to interact, play, and learn with other cultures, especially from India and the local African people. I have experienced discrimination firsthand and am fully aware of the double-edged blade. It can make you stronger, yet at the same time it can also cut right through you, leaving you a haunted figure. I chose the former.

Life gave me the opportunity to travel to over 100 countries, including all of the major wine regions of the world, both for work and pleasure. I experienced the good, the bad and the ugly, met the decadently rich and the pitifully poor, as well as the faultless and the unrepenting guilty characters of life. I found myself in situations where etiquette and the quality of wine reached the heights of perfection and the lowest levels imaginable. I've feasted on a diverse array of food and spices, eaten distinctive meats and vegetables cooked in classical or unique methods, and comfortably fed myself with my hands or other eating utensils, ranging from tree branches to silver cutlery. I have dined with various strata in society, from royals, nobles, and ambassadors to the less privileged. All of these memorable experiences are richly engrained in my memory banks that I now gladly share with you.

Etiquette evolves with life situations and reflects society, and although changes occur, not every aspect of etiquette does. There are important structural keystones of etiquette that remain timeless, unchanged, and respected by all cultures throughout history. Three timeless pillars support the principles of etiquette. I have named them Respect, Courtesy, and Understanding. I term this troika the "Classics of

Etiquette" because they have unwaveringly held a steady course for past, present, and future generations to become well educated in the art of manners and etiquette. Armed with this knowledge, generations can tackle any social situation with a calm demeanour, dignity, and politeness.

You are about to embark on a life-changing experience with etiquette, culture, and wine. By taking the time to understand different situations and environments, you are taking an extraordinarily positive and important step toward supporting global societal harmony.

When different cultures interact, our cultural and etiquette differences become more glaring and noticeable the more time we spend together, but we also can realize how much we have in common. Having drunk wine and broken bread with the titans of the wine world, both as a friend and as a wine and spirit judge, I realized that even at an individual level, this societal phenomenon of differences and commonalities was mirrored. This realization was less of a surprise and more of an affirmation since, after all, individuals make up our society.

This book will share the evolution of etiquette, what it is, and where it is going. I have also shared my diverse experiences within the pages of this book. Through them, we will travel to the world of wine, business, and social activities and hone your etiquette skills in these areas. Through the many scenarios in this book, you will learn the finer points of how to correctly greet others when meeting for the first time, as well as why cultivating these relationships is so important. Discover the secrets of ordering the appropriate bottle of wine for each occasion, and leave your boss suitably impressed with your newly acquired skills when entertaining that very important client. Explore the finer points of high-end dining, whether you are romancing the love of your life or closing off a lucrative business transaction.

In both a social and business context, possessing the insightful scenario knowledge within this book is of immense value. You have in your grasp a chance to increase your personal treasure chest with these rare jewels of knowledge.

We should begin. After you, please—I insist.

PART ONE

Developing Your Personal Etiquette Skills

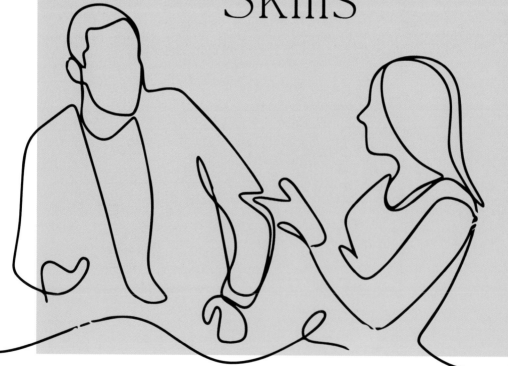

In this chapter, we focus on our personal awareness and flexibility toward other cultures. We train ourselves to be cultural athletes much like we train our intellect by reading and attending institutions of higher education and our bodies by forming healthy habits around food, exercise, and sleep. To grow as cultural athletes, we must acquaint ourselves with and practice the art of etiquette.

There are three key factors you will want to consider: mental acuteness, conversational skills, and social skills. These factors can positively impact and influence your approach to and perception of etiquette in many situations.

DEVELOPING YOUR MENTAL ACUITY

YOU MAY RECALL, with trepidation, examination time at school or university, or perhaps even your driving test. There was anxiety, sweaty palms, sleepless nights of tossing and turning, all because you were unsure of the outcome and dreaded the day. Often, these feelings galvanized you to focus and be single-minded on the examination to come. This focus, concentration, and preparation had you ready for the different ways the examiners might test your level of skill and knowledge.

Sadly, many have of us have lost this honed edge of mental acuity after moving on from those days of intellectual *de rigueur* and succumbing to the monotony of dreary daily duties. Ask any athlete who has trained to reach a goal and then stopped. Their body weakened over time, their flexibility limited, and their stamina reduced.

Our brains are no different. We need to continually develop our mental acuity, as it strengthens our memory, increases concentration, and elevates our level of comprehension and understanding. These qualities are so important when we encounter different scenarios and unfamiliar situations, especially in a cultural context.

Remember, life does not stop, even momentarily, after a test of our skills, so never stop developing your mental acuity.

Build Environmental Awareness

Train yourself to identify the environments that have influenced others. Imagine your friend was born in France. Naturally, it's easy to assume that the prevalent and dominant etiquette practices for your friend would be more aligned with French culture and etiquette. Now add this interesting ingredient: Your friend's heritage and family are from Tunisia, he is a Muslim living with his parents, and he is the first generation born in France. There would certainly be an interlocking of cultures between the old and new countries, as well as generational influences in these circumstances. Being conscious of dual environments gives you the chance to consider the multiple influences impacting your friend's perspective. With this, you are gaining awareness and one of the pillars of the Classics of Etiquette: Understanding.

Situational Awareness

In the previous example, we mentioned the environment of your friend from Tunisia who had a Muslim upbringing. Imagine you are invited to the family home for dinner. Even though you are in a French environment, the situation where you are having dinner is that of a Tunisian family with a Muslim upbringing. Clearly, the etiquette protocols will differ now, and you must make your best effort to respect the etiquette followed at your friend's home.

Every situation, whether formal or informal, is unique. The key is to quickly understand the lay of the land. First, acknowledge your own situation. Yes, you were brought up in a particular way. You are more familiar with certain mannerisms and eating habits, so when confronted with a different set of rules of engagement, it is only natural initially to be puzzled at best and bewildered at worst. Be calm and develop an open mind to each new situation. Be flexible and tap into the Respect pillar of the Classics of Etiquette. To be respectful of the occasion and its significance, identify who carries positions of influence at the gathering, observe the customs, and ultimately ask if you are not sure how to behave. There is no shame when you use intellect in your approach. Applying your developing mental acuity to each new situation is a huge advantage for you, and over time it becomes second nature.

Appreciate the Arts

Unless you have made the triumphant decision to study the arts and culture formally, you, like many of us, probably have a limited understanding of the arts. Arts in this context include paintings, sculpture, and classical music. Immediately you may think of van Gogh, Rembrandt, Picasso, or Monet, who certainly are representative of great artists, but what about Indian, Chinese, Mexican, American, and Canadian artists? If you were asked if you knew of any, I would suspect the answer might be no. There is no shame in that at all.

My suggestion would be to slowly build up your own repertoire and knowledge base by gradually expanding your understanding of artists, sculptors, and cultural creations from other countries. The world of art and culture was not and is not restricted to the "Old World." Expand your mental acuity further by including writers and philosophers from a variety of cultures, and you will be immensely rewarded with this adventure of self-exploration to understand the world around you. This, in turn, makes you more sensitive to other cultures and certainly their etiquette.

Value Other People's Opinions

Opinions and knowledge matter. Since the days of Socrates, Plato, Montesquieu, von Clausewitz, Confucius, and Chanakya, opinions, education, and debate have been highly prized. From the House of Parliament to school halls, we hear opinions and lively debates exchanged. In both the open classrooms held outside under a tree in the stifling African heat and the Ivy League university lecture halls, we observe the passing of knowledge from teacher to student. Acknowledging the opinions of others is valued, but one should do so with logical circumspection.

It is my personal belief that when you enter a person's home, you need to respect their rules and opinions, as it is their home. Similarly, visiting another country is no different. You would expect visitors to your country to respect the rules and beliefs of your country just as they would when visiting your home.

In any unfamiliar situation, I highly recommend you possess an open mind, as you are sure to encounter opinions and beliefs that are very different from your own. Focus your mental acuity by concentrating on the situation you are in. Make efforts to appreciate, absorb, and retain the knowledge and beliefs around you, and this will ensure you develop courtesy and respect, which are both elements of the Classics of Etiquette. This is vitally important and can help you recognize unfamiliar manners and expectations more easily. By valuing these different beliefs, you can elevate your understanding of how others relate to life and how they practice their culture. For example, if you happened to leave your chopsticks upright in the rice during a meal, a Chinese family might frown upon you and stare in disbelief at how disrespectful you are. Careful study and observation in advance could show you that this action is similar to the way they place incense sticks upright in a bowl of rice when paying respect to their ancestors and the dead at a funeral or graveside. Reading is also a great teacher, as reading the correct books can expose you to new beliefs and opinions.

Treasure Literature

There is a reason that great civilizations treasured the priceless value of literature through the ages. It was common amongst different cultures that they recorded the events, discoveries, changes, and the very existence of their society. Through the magic of literature, we can transport our minds to communities of long ago and understand how they evolved and how practices and etiquette changed. If you have a moment of determination and discipline—many claim to have it, but few do—take the time to read the classics of Europe, India, China, Asia, and Africa. Why those countries and continents? In the next two decades, the world's population will be predominantly made up of individuals from those countries. Best you get a head start and know their history, beliefs, and customs. It will be immensely rewarding to your soul and future social interaction.

CULTIVATING CONVERSATIONAL SKILLS

WHEN WE COMMUNICATE, we primarily think it's done verbally. While that may appear to be true, especially when it comes to conversational skills, it is in fact not. We all communicate in various shapes, forms, and styles, such as nonverbal gestures, appearances, and the written form, such as email (page 56).

How we communicate is a matter of significant importance, as it reflects who we are and solidifies what others know about us. The words we use, our gestures and tone, our actions and behaviors are all elements of etiquette, as they can reveal our manners (or lack thereof). Think about the most recent time you felt a gentle or even volcanic rise in anger and disappointment when you were spoken to in what you perceived as an impolite manner. How about when you were ushered in or given a physical command or indication of where to move or go. What caused that reaction? How did those actions make you feel? Cultivating your conversational skills, both verbal and nonverbal, is key to showing good manners.

While practicing those skills, let's not forget an often little-observed aspect of communication: considering who you are talking to. Are you communicating to a person of the same age, older, or younger? And what is your role in this exchange? Consider all of these crucial factors when communicating to others. In certain cultures, more respect is given to the elderly. Even though you may be right in what you are saying, how you say it and the way you say it, as opposed to the singular message, are equally important.

Verbal and Nonverbal

Words can hurt. They can be as painful as a surgeon's scalpel applied to that unanesthetized part of the body where the blade is cutting into you. The pain or anger we experience can be mollified when we know that the person delivering the words may not be doing so in their mother tongue but in their second language. Applying this self-administered knowledge as an anaesthetic can reduce our anxiety and strengthen our understanding.

Understand that meanings for words and phrases can be confusing and different between languages and cultures, so it's very plausible that misinterpretations will occur. Nevertheless, we all should be careful of the words we use. For example, "determined" has a positive connotation while "obstinate" carries a negative connotation, yet both have a similar meaning. Recognizing that a non-native speaker might mix these words paves the way for understanding and peaceful communication.

The silent killer, like a heart attack, is nonverbal communication, which strikes often in ignorance. Ignorance creates chaos and havoc on the etiquette stage. Take the time to learn common international gestures, for example those that are used when greeting others or saying goodbye when leaving and gestures to indicate appreciation of a kindness, gift, or service you may have received. Certain international gestures can be interpreted differently and a seemingly inoffensive sign in one country could well mean the end of a friendship in another.

Both mediums of communication, verbal and nonverbal, demand that the manner in which we communicate is done so with the best of intentions. I advise exercising caution before speaking and also when communicating in a nonverbal manner.

APPEARANCE

The way we dress is another form of conversation, beyond verbal and nonverbal. Think about what your clothing choice "says" to others when you meet. You'll want to make sure that any "talking" that your wardrobe does illuminates you in the best light.

Knowing what to wear, when, and why are the "3 Ws of Appearance" that you may find invaluable. Far too often, we are visually bludgeoned by media channels that suggest being outrageous is fashionable, and that we must dress to shock or draw attention. Certainly, shock and awe have their platform, like modelling runways or certain festivities like the Carnival of Venice and other celebratory events. That is because the "when" and the "why" call for over-the-top dressing.

Over the years, I have found that knowing whom you are meeting and where you will be meeting can influence how you dress appropriately. Then, consider the time (when) and the reason (why) you are meeting. With all this information, you now know what to wear. If you were going to a rodeo in Texas in the United States, wearing a three-piece suit might not be the best choice, just as wearing ripped jeans and a t-shirt to a black-tie opera event in Italy would be out of place. Be mindful to dress for the occasion; neither under dressed nor overdressed, just perfectly dressed, will suffice.

WRITTEN FORM

The art of handwriting is retreating. We don't write or receive many handwritten let-ters these days. The electronic format of emails and texts has made massive advances, and we are constantly facing new abbreviations and acronyms. When I first saw the letters "lol," I interpreted that as "lots of luck" when it really meant "laughing out loud." For BRB, some I know have interpreted this as "bedroom and breakfast," while its actual meaning is "be right back." When using the written form for conversing, whether it is the diminishing handwritten form or the pervasive mode of texts and emails, remember to always be polite, and get your message across in a simple manner. If there's a chance your abbreviations might be misunderstood, take the time to spell them out. Remember whom you are addressing, their cultural situation, and the environment (how the conversation is being presented). Doing so can avoid unnecessary communication problems and future complications.

ACTIVE LISTENING AND OBSERVING

Passive and active listening is infrequently differentiated when broached in conversation. How often do we hear, "I was listening to you" or "I hear you"? Technically yes, you can listen while also texting or having a snack at the same time. Although you may be one of the few that can multitask effectively, it can be very distracting to the other person. In many cultures, it is even disrespectful and plain rude to multitask while others are communicating with you. This kind of passive listening shows disinterest in others. Develop the importance of active listening by using your focus and body language to show a person you are solely interested in what they are talking to you about. You will reap the benefits from the appreciation and engagement of your conversational partner. In some cultures, active listening means you need to look them in the eye when shaking hands, and in others it is necessary to look aside slightly and not directly into their eye. It is all etiquette. Developing this listening habit is an investment in yourself that will serve you graciously and magnanimously in the future as a well-mannered individual.

ENGAGE IN APPROPRIATE CONVERSATIONAL TOPICS WITH STRANGERS

Certain topics are taboo in some cultures but quite common and carefree in others. For example, when meeting someone for the first time, they may be curious about you, wanting to know where you were born, what you do for a living, and what your interests are. These types of questions can appear unchallenging and not even mildly intimidating, but when the questions move on to your personal status, things can become uncomfortable. Imagine being asked if you are married, divorced, or single, how much money you make, and what your political affiliation is. These may prove more of a challenge, so avoid using them yourself and anticipate that these types of questions might come up so you can be prepared for the unexpected. Keep in mind that different generations have differing views on what is considered inappropriate or not, so it is important to consider the generation asking the question and the generation being asked the question.

There are many conversational topics that one can engage in, certainly amongst very close friends. For initial meetings and until one is more comfortable, there are certain topics to avoid. My suggestion is to skip discussions about politics, religion, age, sexual orientation, and money. Prepare yourself for small talk by having a few topics in mind that you are more comfortable and *au fait* with discussing. The broader and more diverse those topics are, the more versatile you become in meeting and engaging people. In my experience, topics like food, music, art, and personal travel stories (both good and bad) are excellent options. Remember, they may also be as unpracticed in the art of etiquette and social niceties as you are. Do not feel intimidated.

UNDERSTANDING RELATIONSHIPS

Cultivating conversational skills is an art that begins with a canvas of understanding your environment. Knowing the environment, including the relationship you have with those around you, will dictate how you communicate and in what manner. Relationships are imperative in all cultures. The age factor and the hierarchical status of whom you are talking to all play a role. Understanding relationships is extremely important in Asian culture where status is not based solely on wealth but on a plethora of other factors like age, education, cross family relations, allegiance, and deeds performed in the past.

Every country has a distinct set of rules and guidelines pertaining to relationships. For example, in England (in most cases) if you say "someone is my sister," it can be assumed that you both have the same father and mother, a blood sister in essence. In many other cultures, like India and China, a person called sister could technically be a cousin. This "sister" might even be a very close friend whom they have known for decades. This loose affiliation can also apply to uncles and aunts. So, always consider the situation, and don't let the familial title used deceive you. The titles are often simply used as a sign of respect.

By understanding a person's hierarchical position in certain cultures, especially in the Middle East, Africa, and Asia, you can address people correctly and choose appropriate conversational topics to engage in.

Respect the Situation and Environment

Out of all the crucial factors to gauge with etiquette, assessing the situation and the broad environmental framework you are in is key. I have repeated the important duo of "situation and environment" frequently in the book, and it is because it is so definitively important, even for conversational skills.

You might be in England, enjoying a stay in London, a very cosmopolitan city, then visit a rural English town where their traditions and manners will differ vastly from those in London. You cannot be expected to know all, or half, or even a small fraction of the entire world's different etiquette and foibles, but you can still be courteous when communicating. Adding your personal touch of politeness in the form of a clean-cut appearance, respectful words, and careful gestures can make conversing in both environments so much more interesting and appealing for you and the residents.

If you find yourself in a situation or environment with customs that make you uncomfortable, you can choose not to follow them if you express yourself respectfully. Some countries do not permit men and women to eat together or require that no meat is to be eaten on Fridays. With these differences, it is up to us to follow or politely refuse. The choice is yours, but if you decide to not follow the etiquette of the house, please decline graciously and excuse yourself without creating an awkward or embarrassing situation. You can prepare for these conversations by learning and practicing polite phrases that are accepted in that environment.

For example, these phrases may be useful and adaptable for various situations. "I appreciate the hospitality you have shown me. I apologize that I won't be able to follow that particular etiquette. Please excuse me while I step out for a while and I can return after you have ended your session."

"Thank you for your understanding, but I'm afraid I won't be able to follow this particular etiquette practice. Please excuse me while I go back to my room."

"I apologize for any inconvenience this may cause, but I'm unable to follow the etiquette exercised at this time. Please allow me to excuse myself and find a quiet space."

In the future, if you know you cannot accept certain practices, you can also refrain from visiting or placing yourself in such situations.

ACQUIRING SOCIAL SKILLS

SOCIAL SKILLS ENCOMPASS all of our different personal facets when meeting the outside world. Are we approachable? Do we appear warm and pleasant? Do people perceive us as someone they would want to know better? How do people see us upon first meeting? Your social skills play a part in all of those perceptions. In Asia, upon first meeting, don't be surprised if others scrutinize the way you dress from head to toe. This is the first test that you may face, and there are many more. The big test, of course, is when you speak.

Our primary social skills relate to our language and behavior. We observe how people act and react, take note of the way they speak and listen, and have an overall awareness of situations both locally and globally. Believe me, others are also observing you in the same meticulous manner. To be aware is to be forewarned, and this means to be prepared. Acquiring a solid set of social skills will help you immensely in developing good manners, understanding correct etiquette, and being able to maneuver the different cultural and social environments.

AWARENESS OF GLOBAL TRENDS

To build an awareness of global trends, you must read, read, and read. Whether it is the standard newspaper, online tabloids, or social media, each and every one of these sources has mountains of information. Take some time to sift through, analyze, and see what is important, disregarding the rest. When you use this information to discuss these topics with others, you can strengthen your social skills while learning about the latest trends and what is happening in the world.

Trends are not just related to fashion, but also to social interaction and etiquette. Think about Zoom, the online meeting software that was catapulted to prominence during the COVID-19 pandemic lockdown period. Before the pandemic, it was socially more acceptable to take the time to meet in person for both social and business engagements. Currently, holding a Zoom meeting is not considered impolite at all, and in fact, is thought to be proper for several reasons. By holding such meetings, the carbon footprint of travelling is reduced, time is saved, and greater flexibility is made available.

You may agree or disagree with trends, but it is important to be aware of what is happening in the world around you. This can make interacting with different people less arduous a task and, in certain instances, very enjoyable. Knowledge is power.

Emotional Attractiveness

This absolutely ignores physical attractiveness. It relates specifically to your composure and demeanor, and it takes into consideration your ability to connect with others on either an intellectual or spiritual basis. If it is easy to bond with others, your emotional attractiveness is considered more appealing, and it is so much easier for you to relate with others.

Do you recall a time you first met someone and within an instant you felt there was no possibility of bonding then, nor would there ever be? Yet, at times you can bond closely with someone you have just met. It happens all the time, when we attend a meeting, a master class, a presentation, or a meal at a conference table. There are countless situations where we meet different people and we know deep inside if a bonding will occur or not. All this can be attributable to each other's emotional attractiveness.

By developing your social skills, you increase your emotional attractiveness. The more you interact, the more confident you become. This is because meeting and connecting with others becomes easier the more you do it, and so your level of social comfort increases greatly. All of this has the effect of increasing your emotional attractiveness.

EMOTIONAL QUOTIENT

Emotional quotient (EQ) or intelligence is a measurement of your ability to understand and reflect on the emotions of others and yourself. Having an elevated level of emotional attractiveness gives you a higher EQ score. By working on your emotional attractiveness, you can develop and grow your EQ score. It has been empirically proven that having a higher EQ can assist one in developing relationships and building rapport with others while reducing conflict and stress.

To increase our emotional quotient, we need to understand the individual: their character, their values, and what is important to them. To do this, we must consider the society and values they grew up with. For example, in North America, we are bombarded in the media with scenes showcasing holidays in exotic and romantic faraway places, succulent meals in restaurants, luxurious cars, clothing, and palatial homes. All of this is culturally indicative of success. But consider the keen angler in a developing country enjoying his time awaiting the catch of the day. We cannot apply the glamour, glitz, and trappings of success as North Americans might view it to his idea of a successful life. He may want to live more simply. By understanding him as an individual, we show empathy, which helps our EQ grow.

In summary, emotional attractiveness, the ease with which we connect to others, is measured by the emotional quotient. Empathy is the actual application of "putting yourself into the other person's situation" and simply understanding them. Empathy will not only develop your EQ and emotional attractiveness, but also help you strengthen your social skills.

Awareness of Generational Perspectives

Unquestionably, different generations see life differently, live life differently, and value life differently. Life and wine are similar. A mature wine, when consumed, will express a different taste, flavor, and nose compared to the younger wine. Each vintage, each generation, is different. Acknowledging these differences allows you to appreciate each vintage, just as embracing generational differences offers unique socializing opportunities.

Older generations may wish to cling to their past days of glory, recalling achievements they attained and resting on their memories. The younger generations are charged with the exuberance of youth and the desire to achieve, create, and make their mark in this world. All generations should be aware of the changing times and these differences, as reflected by fashion, food, style, and etiquette. All generations need to show empathy toward one another. We should be sensitive to each other in a caring and understanding manner.

The younger generations should consider that, for the older generations, the world they grew up in is disappearing daily in front of their eyes. In certain cases, parts have totally disappeared, like the rotary phone and cassette players. The older generations also need to understand and embrace the younger generation. The new generation lives in a new world where everything is fresh with many "firsts" in life. Their two worlds are different, like rotary phones to smart phones. Finding ways to bridge those different worlds will build your social skills.

Part One Summary

Etiquette changes with context but certain aspects remain. The classics like "thank you" and "please" will always remain, as do the pillars of Respect, Courtesy, and Understanding, and these form the structure of a polite and civil society. "Hey" may be the new form of greeting as opposed to "good morning" or "how do you do," but the intention is the same: a warm greeting.

You will encounter in your life innumerable situations that call for good manners, and I would not be brave enough to attempt to quantify them. The situations I provide are also not exhaustive, but they do have a common theme in them all: pragmaticism.

You may agree or disagree with the suggestions offered, and that is perfectly fine, as they are mine based on my personal experience and travels. It is my hope that by considering these suggestions, your future experiences in life be smooth and heartwarming so they can be added to the list of priceless adventures you have already accumulated in your personal treasure chest of life.

Remember, always understand the environment and situation you are in, local customs, and the expectations between the different ages and sexes. They may well differ from where you grew up and currently live. So be aware and respectful when you visit other countries and homes. Always exercise courtesy, be respectful, and show a great deal of patience and kindness. Let's take the next step in our adventure now with scenario-specific etiquette.

PART TWO

Scenario-Specific Etiquette

There are four sections to Part Two of this book. We shall navigate through different situations together. Some of these scenarios you may encounter more frequently and others less so.

In section one, you will learn the importance of greeting people correctly when meeting for the first time. You'll also learn what gifts to bring and colors to ignore, how to sit appropriately in the lounge, and how to correct a mistake if you have made one.

In section two, you will travel to the world of wine and spirits. Enhance your tasting and evaluation skills. Build a level of comfort for yourself when it comes to selecting wines and pairing food with wine. Whatever the scenario, your skills and mannerisms will be professional and poised.

In section three, the magnificent gathering for food is always a delight. Knowing where to sit, what order to use the cutlery, and how to interact at dinner with others is vitally important. If you must eat lobsters and oysters, you will learn how to eat them elegantly. All these pearls of wisdom are yours in this section.

In section four, you discover the art of business by showing yourself in the best possible light. Learn to appreciate different cultural habits, minimize offensive situations, and cultivate the nuances of the finer points of negotiating with different characters. Prepare for the taboo topics and questions you may be asked. All this awaits you in this section.

After having read all four sections, you will be able to assert yourself in a positive light with friends, business colleagues, and other professionals. Most important of all, through your good manners, you will be leaving a positive and lasting impression. You will come across many useful tips, advice, and examples that will ensure your social interactions are more engaging, delightful, and productive.

SOCIAL GREETING AND MEETING ETIQUETTE

IN THIS SECTION, you will learn to understand and master the intricacies of social etiquette from the first invitation and handshake to the final farewell. You will be equipped with the knowledge and skills to know what is expected of you and what types of behavior are frowned upon. The knowledge you acquire will increase your confidence to maneuver within multiple social situations with composure and professionalism. Discover the appropriate way to introduce yourself and others in a variety of settings, how to make small talk that leads to meaningful conversations, and how to diplomatically deal with cultural differences.

Let's begin by communicating. The first step in communicating when you meet someone is the greeting. Take this analogy of a little acorn as an example of how communication grows from that first step. We shall call the little acorn "Greeting." If we nurture Greeting and care for it, then Greeting will develop into a huge oak tree called "Friendship." How we nurture it, when we nurture it, and the way we nurture it will define the Friendship's strength. To be able to understand the intricacies that life places in front of our path, and to know the different ways diverse cultures greet one another, is the first step of planting that little acorn.

Let's go and meet some people now.

The Personality of a Handshake: How Firm Should Your Grip Be?

Some claim that the personality of your handshake is reflective of you. If the grasp of your handshake tends to be a vice-like grip, it gives an immediate impression to the other party that you are an overpowering personality. If, on the other hand, you have a somewhat limp grip, like a dying fish grasping for life, or allow the back of the other person's hand to be facing skywards while yours is in the earthly downward direction, you are showing weakness. The best method is to have the shaking hand of both parties parallel to the ground. The grip should be firm, but not hard or limp. Then there are the eyes. Do you look at the person with whom you are shaking hands directly or not?

In Japan, while the handshake is certainly not aggressive, it tends to be somewhat on a more passive and firm scale, and they don't look directly at you. There is minimal eye contact. Americans tend to have a firm handshake with direct eye contact, and they generally shake hands in two up and down motions. Any longer is considered a waste of time. In China, the grip is somewhat lighter but firm, and then you hold on to the other person's hand a second or two longer after the handshake has been completed. They tend not to look directly into each other's eyes. In Russia, you don't shake the hand of the opposite sex, and at times it's even considered impolite. It's more traditional for a man to kiss a woman's hand rather than shaking it when you greet them. In North America, both men and women tend to adopt the strong handshake practice, while women from India and parts of Southeast Asia rarely shake hands at all with men. They gesture by putting hands together in a prayer-like gesture called "namaste" in India, "wai" in Thailand, "sampeah" in Cambodia, and "nop" in Laos. In South Korea, you need to use your left hand to hold your right hand as you shake hands with the other party. This is an immensely respectful gesture to the other party.

Whichever way you choose to greet others, ensure that you extend the sincerity of your character.

How Do You Introduce Yourself?

Whether it's a kiss, handshake, bow, nod, or a combination, it is advisable that you know which one to apply. If you get it wrong, the least damage you might suffer is an awkward grimace. At worst, you may receive a total rebuff and be labeled as ill-prepared and insensitive. Avoid having the proverbial egg on your face by making sure you know how to introduce yourself correctly.

During my visit to Mendoza, Argentina, a handshake and a nod was quite acceptable during the first meeting. On subsequent meetings, it was common to greet with an embrace between males and an "air kiss" on the cheek for female friends. In Chile, shaking hands is the norm, but with subsequent meetings, male colleagues could pat one another on the back or shoulder.

In Italy, shaking hands is common and, as I discovered at the Vinitaly Expo in Verona, done very enthusiastically. There it is expected that you shake hands when you are introduced and when you leave. You can also grasp the arm of the other person with your other hand that is free. It was recommended for men not to shake hands with the ladies unless they extended their hand out first.

In Japan, a handshake is appropriate, as they do follow and are aware of Western greeting styles, but they also tend to bow. This is a highly regarded greeting that shows respect and is appreciated. Normally, to show courtesy, a slight bow is given. If someone bows to greet you and they are of the same status as you, the corresponding bow by you should be the same depth. The depth of a bow indicates the status of the one you are bowing to: The lower the bow, the greater the status. In China, if you are being introduced to a crowd, they may applaud you in which case you should applaud back. They will either shake hands or nod, but not bow to you.

Another important fact to remember is that there is also a particular order to follow when you are greeting people. It's best not to randomly greet people at a gathering. Always introduce or expect to be introduced to the most senior ranking person present first in the business setting or the eldest first at a social gathering. The question is do you bow, kiss, or shake the hands? Every country is different, so asking the locals beforehand is a wise move. Observe how others greet, and don't forget to smile.

India is unquestionably the fast-track economic tiger on the global scale. Its citizens are traveling across the globe, and millions of them are highly qualified. They are leaving India to immigrate, to do business, or just to travel. To acquaint yourself with one of the most populous greetings in the world would be an asset for you, as it has been for me over the years. It will become even more important as the years roll on by.

For ten years of my early life, I grew up within a Gujarati community where I learned many of their customs and greetings. The art and action of clasping your hands then adding a bow, a nod, and saying the words "namaste" is widely used in Southeast Asia. The word "namas" originates from Sanskrit, meaning "I bow," while the greeting "te" translates "to you." Combining these two words becomes "namaste," which means "I bow to you."

The spiritual implication is that within each of us there is a divine being, and the "namaste" greeting is acknowledging that divinity within us as a sign of respect. Therefore, when you're meeting someone and you bow, nod and clasp your hands saying "namaste," you are, in essence, bowing to that divine being residing within that other person. The gesture is to encourage peace, harmony, and mutual respect between the two minds meeting. There are fewer examples of deeper respect than the "namaste" greeting.

It is my belief that if we were to all employ a greater sense of dignity and add the ingredients of respect and kindness, we would all be living in a more peaceful world that is less predatory and less skewed towards conflict, selfish behavior, and poor etiquette.

Should You Introduce Yourself to Others?

The clinking of the glasses. The heavy soundless footsteps on the plush carpet. The occasional laughter and awkward bump as you stand at a cocktail party, alone. Or was it the trade gathering where you were on your own and all your colleagues abandoned you? Many of us are familiar with this rather lonely scenario and have had to endure this. Why? You need only introduce yourself.

We want to meet more people so we can broaden our circle of influence and societal boundaries. It's natural when we begin our careers to do so. Whether it is at trade events, cocktail parties, stand-up events, networking, or meet-up groups, we must introduce ourselves to meet people.

If you are at a trade show, the most opportune place for introductions is where the attendees gather at the high tables nibbling on a quick snack and having a quick drink in between visiting the booths. This is a brief respite from the trudging and bumping, so introducing yourself at this time is the easiest. For example, a simple "Hello, my name is John. How are you finding the wine festival? Any recommendations?" In my many years, this breaks the ice with ease and grace. After a while, if you feel you would like to pursue this new connection, then exchange a business card. This is what these trade shows are all about. You are in business, and business is all about relationships, so go and develop them!

Cocktail parties can appear more intimidating, given the often lavish settings, but don't be put off. One needs to be more circumspect as to when to approach and whom to approach. My suggestion is to look out for single individuals who are hovering around looking lonely, bored, or both. Or you can identify the liveliest person, as chances are they know literally everyone present and can introduce you to others. Be confident, smile when you greet the person you have chosen to approach, and do so at an opportune moment, not when they are in the middle of a conversation or introducing others. Business and social gatherings are places where you can introduce yourself to others, but there are other less common scenarios.

One of the strangest places that I have found myself exchanging introductions was while standing in the long, laboriously time-consuming queues at several tourist attractions in Europe. You are standing next to someone for possibly thirty minutes or more. If they look interesting enough, I don't see any harm in introducing yourself and having a quick chat. You have a common bond: You are visiting the same attraction.

From one of these encounters, I found and have continued to nurture a life-long friendship with a fellow wine professional.

In Europe, North America, and South America, it is perhaps easier to offer an introduction among fairly socially outgoing communities. In other cultures, especially those in Asia, it might be somewhat more difficult to approach others, as they are somewhat more reserved. Remember your situation and environment to guide your actions. Knowing when to introduce yourself is etiquette.

Coming back to the question of if you should introduce yourself to others, the answer is a definitive, yes! You should. There are exceptions. I would hesitate to do so at a formal gathering where the hosts generally provide introductions. Apart from formal events, it is encouraged to interact at social gatherings, which means introducing yourself. It is a social after all.

How to Introduce Yourself to a Group

So, now that you have managed to get your foot into the door, you are facing a group of two or three individuals. Someone says to you, "Tell us about yourself." What do you say? What do you do? Do not panic. Be calm. Evaluate the situation: Is this more of a social or business setting?

If you are in a quasi-business setting when you are asked to introduce yourself, a standard introduction could sound like this, "Hello everybody, my name is XYZ. I work for ABC. I am visiting this beautiful city 123 for the purposes of this tradeshow for a few days." It is very practical and clinical. Your new acquaintances know nothing about you except your name and for whom you work. While this is a good start, it can be rather boring, so I would suggest you end your introduction with something unique to yourself. Make sure there is a memorable point, aspect, or feature they will remember about you. If you are required to give a short introduction of yourself to a large group in a formal organization, limiting yourself to your name, what you do, for how long, your experience, and other skills you possess is adequate. For a small organization without big corporate culture, you can be less formal and introduce elements of yourself, as well as your professional side, just as you might during a small group conversation.

Social events are far easier and more relaxed. This allows everyone to share more interesting insights about themselves, and you get to know others away from a business perspective. When you are introducing yourself, remember to look at more than one person, scanning the group. After your introduction, it is the best time to ask the person who requested your introduction to do the same.

It's always beneficial to have a rehearsed and well-practiced speech that can encapsulate aspects of you that are not solely related to your business. My suggestion: Practice your introduction for each type of setting.

How to Introduce Your Guests When You Host

With wine, there is an order in which to drink it. White before red, young before old, and dry before sweet. When introducing people, always introduce the younger to the older, the lower ranked to the higher ranked, and people you know the least about to the people you know the most about. This process works quite smoothly and is practiced etiquette.

In business circles, when you are the host introducing two people who have never met each other, there is a certain accepted etiquette to follow. For example, imagine Mr. A. is the senior marketing development officer for Company XYZ, and Miss B is the CEO of company 123. Given their stature in the business world, one would introduce Mr. A. to Miss B. The person with the lower status or position is always introduced to the upper-level position. In this case, the CEO is the highest ranked person in the company.

When you introduce people as a host, you should always clearly state the name of the person you are introducing, the introduction itself, then a brief introduction on the person that includes their position and what they do. Then you repeat the process for the other party. For example, "May I introduce Miss. BB to you, Mr. Dirk. She is with East West Import Company and is the export director. Mr. Dirk, allow me to introduce you to Miss. BB. Henry is the import director of Blue Light Manufacturing. I am sure you will both have many things to discuss. Enjoy your evening, and please excuse me. I must greet our other guests."

When introducing friends, colleagues, or family members to each other at an informal gathering, it is advisable to introduce the person you have known for the shortest time or know the least about to another person you have a closer relationship with and know more about. When introducing one person to a group, address the group and then introduce the person. For example, "President Sanchez and board members, I would like to introduce Cambridge professor Mr. Ken Harold to you." By addressing the group in this fashion, you have their undivided attention and it makes the rest of the introductions easier.

Introductions are far too often casually set aside. They should not be, as introductions are particularly important in many different cultures.

How to Introduce Yourself to People Older Than You

From an incredibly early age, I often heard my late mother tell me, "A great man has a great heart." She kept reminding me of that phrase. The reason I mention that is because it's very true. Having read countless biographies and met so many extraordinary and remarkable people in my life, there was a common bond I discovered they all possessed. Each had a large portion of humane kindness in their character. I am grateful for her teachings, as my mother's experience has benefitted me greatly. My one proviso is that it should be a great "person" rather than "man."

I would now like to share again with you a phrase that keeps coming up in this book: "Assess the situation and environment you are in." By understanding and correctly interpreting your surroundings and circumstances, only then can you act accordingly with respect, kindness, and grace. It is, after all, part of the etiquette equation. By knowing where you are, you realize how to behave correctly. This is especially true when interacting with older generations, as they are treated differently in each culture.

With greetings in Southeast and Central Asia, more deference is paid to the elderly. Whether it is in business meetings or social gatherings, elders are respected greatly. They are seated first and eat first, whereas everyone else at the dinner table waits politely for them before starting on their own meal. When greeting elders in India, some may reach down and touch the ground where the elders stand or touch the elder person's feet. In Greece, they address the older people by their name and last name, not just their first name. In Mexico, you can use an honorific like Don, which is the equivalent of Sir, or Doña, which means Madame. In Japan and Thailand, there are specific words used in their languages when greeting older people and younger people. In South Africa, when shaking hands with the elders, one should use both hands, while in Zambia, if the elders are seated, then you must go down on one knee and then shake their hands.

This deference towards the elderly is not universal and cultures differ. In the United States, greetings are generally more informal and, while it can vary by family, there is not an American cultural expectation of special treatment when meeting older people.

As always, be cognizant of the prevailing environment. It is best to observe, absorb, and follow. There is a Chinese saying that if you have an older person within your family, you have a jewel and a treasure. They have experienced so much. They can be a voice of wisdom for the benefit of those seeking it. We all will become old one day.

Who Should You Greet First at an Informal Gathering?

Your main target for greetings is always the hosts. If you were invited by a friend and don't know who the hosts are, then ask your friend to introduce the hosts to you as soon as you arrive.

Thereafter, there are three main options while you are at the party. One strategy is to remain like the "Scarlet Pimpernel" and hug the curtain line, watching and observing. Then once you identify who you want to meet, you make your move like a predatory African cheetah.

The second option is the fast-moving school of fish strategy. Fish change their course easily; you could replicate these changes in the social current. You will meet as many people as possible, in no specific order. This method favors the quantity of people you meet. I would not say this favors quantity over quality, as I am sure all the guests present have something unique to offer.

The third option is your own, which could be a combination of both. In my experience, you can only meet so many people at a gathering. Time is limited, so if you really want to meet people, then make it worth your while. Be selective in the hope that an enduring and meaningful friendship can develop, rather than the perfunctory hello and goodbye.

Determine which style you are more comfortable with at an informal gathering. Oftentimes, these events can be quite animated, loud, and difficult to interact at, which has limitations. Always be respectful to yourself and others when meeting for the first time.

When Invited to a Gathering, What is Expected of You Before Attending?

Who does not like a party? We all do. When we receive an invitation to a party or event, we should appreciate and value the fact that it is truly a privilege to have been invited. So, it is very important to consider certain details before attending, like what is the purpose of the gathering, what time is it, and where is the venue? Then, you can prepare the appropriate gift if one is required, and you can dress appropriately for the event. Knowing what time you are expected to arrive and if there is a specific time the party ends makes your time management more efficient.

Formal invitations will clearly state who is being invited, why, when, and where the event is being held, what the dress code is, and who is hosting. The invitation will also provide instructions on how to RSVP, which is an abbreviation for the French phrase "*répondez s'il vous plaît.*" Translated into English it means "please respond, thank you." Above all, always RSVP. When you reply, use the same method the invitation extended to you. RSVP as early as possible to allow the organizer as much time as possible to finalize their event.

For informal events, it is equally important to know as much information as possible. As mentioned earlier, the time, venue, date, and reason for the gathering are usually provided, but you may need to confirm if there is a dress code. You do not want to be overdressed or underdressed for the occasion. Imagine dressing up in a suit and tie looking like James Bond at an informal BBQ lunch gathering. That would be overkill. Equally, wearing tattered, but fashionable, holes-in-the-knees jeans would be savagely underdressed for a dinner event.

If the gathering is a potluck event, confirm if you will be required to bring anything. This type of event usually involves people bringing a special dish of their choosing to the gathering. For a potluck, it is always wise to know how many people you need to cater for and if there are any guest allergies to keep in mind.

We have covered purpose, dress requirements, gifts, timing, and, in the case of a potluck, what food you should bring. The final piece of advice is to enjoy yourself and have a wonderful and memorable evening with friends.

What Is Expected of You When You Arrive and During a Gathering?

If the gathering is formal, the hosts will be at the door to greet you. Then someone else might escort you and introduce you to other guests who are attending the party. Many guests enjoy meeting new people at a party. People are curious—it's in our nature—so be prepared for questions. Obvious questions may include, how do you know the hosts of the event? What is your profession? What do you do for a living and where do you live? What are your hobbies and interests? Also be prepared for questions that might make you uncomfortable and have your own plan as to how to respond.

In a formal dinner, there is generally a short period when people will mingle around, have a cocktail or glass of wine, and engage in light conversation. There may very well be sparkling wine and hors d'oeuvres being served. Don't forget to hold your flute glass correctly by the stem of the glass. Remember to wipe your mouth with a napkin after nibbling on hors d'oeuvres before sipping your drink. If not, you will leave unsightly greasy marks on the rim of the glass. Shortly after the mingling, you will be directed to your seat. Normally there will be a name card indicating your seat. If there are no name cards, await the host and see if they have a preferred seating arrangement. Either way, follow the instructions that the hosts give. If you are with a lady companion, it would be gracious of you to offer to pull the chair out for her. If they would like that, then please do so. If they decline, then proceed to seat yourself.

If the event is informal, such as a BBQ or having dinner around the kitchen table on a Sunday night, it will likely be more relaxed. Even when the event is less formal, you will most likely still be greeted by the host. If you are greeted by a fellow guest, ask where the host is. In this situation, go immediately to where the hosts are and greet them to let them know you have arrived and ask if you can help them in any way. Drinks are normally "help yourself" at these events if it is not a seated dinner. At an impromptu gathering, my best advice would be to go with the flow of the evening. Observe the mood and style of the other guests and the hosts. Appreciate the wonderful bonding and mood of friendship, food, and wine and enjoy the evening for what it is.

At all events, it is quite possible you may bump into a friend or acquaintance. You might be required to introduce the person who accompanied you to the event to new friends and others at the gathering. Ensure you know the correct etiquette for introducing people (page 38).

To summarize, always greet the hosts of the party upon arrival. Settle in discreetly with poise and elegance, hold your wine glass correctly, and know where to sit. Above all, be kind, respectful, and courteous to other guests.

Should You Always Arrive on Time for a Party?

There are certain events you cannot arrive late for. A tee time at the golf course is one of those events, and your own wedding is another. When we think about what time we should arrive at parties, there are several factors to keep in mind. Arriving at a party early can be stressful for the hosts, as they are still preparing, so for some parts of the world, arriving later is more acceptable.

In South America, it is not considered impolite if you arrive maybe even up to thirty minutes or more later than the time stated. In North America, if you arrive within fifteen minutes of the time you were asked to come to the party, it is still considered acceptable. More than fifteen minutes late would be considered impolite. If that were to happen, I would strongly recommend that you inform your hosts that you will be late (page 44). Arriving later than the fifteen-minute grace period would be disrespectful to the hosts, so making the courteous call can prevent starting off the evening with your host feeling bitter. The best time is to arrive on time in both continents.

Over the years, I have been blessed with a circle of friends that has encompassed many diverse cultures and nationalities. Within that circle, I have many Indian and Chinese friends. They have shared with me that to arrive on time in their culture is unheard of. I can substantiate this from personal experience. Whenever I have a party, my Indian and Chinese friends are always the last to arrive. It is more the norm than the exception that they will arrive later than the requested time. It is not unusual to arrive even an hour later.

As stated, there are certain events you cannot be late for. If it is a formal event like a wedding, anniversary, or graduation, it is highly recommended that you arrive on time. That would be my wisest advice, as arriving late can be disruptive and embarrassing. If it is a less formal or simple gathering, I think the fifteen-minute rule would be quite acceptable. Oh, by the way, do not forget to bring a gift.

Having travelled to Greece, Spain, and the Philippines, I can attest that lateness extends to other meetings and appointments in life, not just parties. Think about that when you do get invited to parties or must attend meetings in other countries. My experience in South Africa is that people are late for parties and appointments. There is a phrase they use called "now" with three different meanings, depending how it is used. If someone says "now" it means "sure, I will get around to it hopefully." "Just now" means later, and "now, now" means "I will see you pretty soon."

Some will say better late than never, but personally, I advise to not be too late when leaving or arriving.

If You Are Late for a Gathering, What Should You Do?

As soon as you know that you will be late for the event, you need to let the hosts of the event know, especially if you are the guest of honor or the main guest for that evening. Everyone is waiting to see you.

Even if you aren't the guest of honor, there are many reasons why you should inform the hosts if you will be late. Late arrivals of expected guests can often cause anxiety for hosts; they worry that you are lost, experiencing transport problems, or involved in an accident. The hosts may have a special evening planned that has several events scheduled for the night and entertainment that they wish to start on time. It could be a special dish that they will only prepare ten minutes before all of the guests arrive. The list of reasons is endless, but the sentiment is the same: Being courteous and considerate not only to the hosts, but also to all of the other guests, is good etiquette.

So, if you know a day or two in advance that you will be late, inform the organizer of the event sooner rather than later. They will appreciate that greatly. If, on the day of the event, you realize you will be late for any reason, call or text to let the hosts know that you will be late and what time you anticipate arriving. If you cannot contact them, then try and contact someone that you know will also be attending the event so that they can tell the host and hostess. You will then have done all that is required. As a special touch, you could be gracious enough to let the host know that they should carry on without you, so as not to inconvenience the other guests and the evening, and you will be happy to join in when you arrive. It is better to travel safely and arrive a few minutes late than not at all.

Business meetings are notorious for running late, and excuses are often given by both parties. It happens. There might be traffic snarl-ups, accidents, other meetings running late, and even more delays you cannot imagine. The same etiquette practices apply: Inform the other business party of your lateness just as you would do with hosts of a party.

However, to try to prevent the lateness, I suggest that before agreeing to a business meeting, you should ensure that the timing is practical in terms of travel time, rush hour considerations, and parking availability.

If you are late for a play or opera performance, you will need to understand that you may not be allowed into the performance until there is an intermission. So timing is key, but even the best of us sometimes arrive late.

What is Expected of You at the End of or After the Party or Gathering?

Do not leave the party too soon. If the party is open-ended without a leave-by time, then plan to spend at least two hours there before deciding to leave. Leaving too soon leaves a poor impression of you with others and may give them the idea that something was wrong with the party and you did not enjoy yourself. Even if that is true, there is no need to advertise it. After deciding to leave, do so discreetly with minimal fanfare.

Before you leave, show good manners by saying goodbye to the hosts. If this is impossible because of a huge line of people waiting to say goodbye to the hosts and you cannot wait, at least inform someone close to the hosts to pass on a goodbye message. You might say, "Please thank them for a lovely evening and let them know that unfortunately we weren't able to say goodbye, but we will be contacting them in the next day or so." You don't have to say goodbye to everyone at the event, but you should strive to speak to the hosts one last time.

If you are at a restaurant, pay your share of the cost for the evening. Do not leave without making sure that your share is taken care of. Ensure that everyone can get home safely by asking, if it is convenient, if anyone needs a lift to a nearby station or drop-off point. Your graciousness will be appreciated and remembered. Many of us can recall our student days when we did not have a car and hoped someone would be kind enough to offer. I can remember many occasions when I was fortunate enough for someone to offer me a lift.

If the event was an impromptu gathering or dinner by the kitchen table, do offer to help the hosts clear up after the meal or see if there is any other way you could be of assistance. The most likely response by the host will be to say, "That's kind. No thank you. Please go and relax." Whether they accept your offer or not, your courtesy and kindness will be appreciated.

If it's a very formal event you attended, you should mail (not email) a handwritten letter thanking them for the lovely evening. Mail it to the hosts the next day. This is the preferred way for formal events. For the less formal events, email is more prevalent these days, but at the very least sending a text or even making a phone call are acceptable. Always consider the situation and environment when sending the thank you message, as it does reflect upon you as a person.

One final piece of advice: Visit the bathroom before leaving for home. Then there will be no pressure to rush the trip going home.

How Should You Dress When You Visit Someone's Home for the First Time?

Regardless of where you are going, it is universally understood that leaving your home and going outside in public, there is still a modicum of expectation when it comes to the dress code. Obviously, if we are going out to the supermarket, popping out to the gas station, or stopping at the corner shop to get some bread and milk, the dress code could be described as very casual. The basic rule is having clean, not necessarily crisply ironed, clothes.

Certainly, wearing clean clothes is the minimum standard and appreciated. In certain countries, until it became fashionable to wear torn jeans and threaded tops, no one would dare wear clothes with holes and patches in public. Every country has their expectations, and when you travel, you need to know that dressing appropriately is respecting yourself and others around you.

Dress is incredibly significant because it is indicative of how you respect yourself and those you will be meeting or visiting. It is very important for you to know who will be present. Ask who will be attending, what is the purpose of the gathering, and if there is a dress code. By doing so you will eliminate any potential embarrassment. If there is no dress code, then I strongly suggest smart casual, as that is the chameleon of all dress codes.

Be careful of wearing certain colors on certain occasions. Red is associated with purity in India, raises the danger and caution signals in the Middle East, and reflects happiness and good luck in China. Another consideration when dressing up is the type of accessories you will wear. Care should be taken to consider if what you are wearing is deemed "cultural appropriation." Karlie Kloss, a Victoria's Secret model, wore a Native American headdress and many thought this was insensitive. When you are visiting someone's home, it is a huge privilege, as they are opening their private sanctuary—their home—to you. At the very least your clothes should not be offensive in taste, be clean, and smell pleasant.

When you are dressing up for a first-time meeting with your significant other's parents at their home, this has a more serious tone. May I suggest a more conventional approach, unless you know something to the contrary. Remember, your clothes reflect you, and if you are serious about the relationship, it is important to give a good first impression. Perhaps ask your significant other if their parents are particular about "what not to wear." First impressions always count.

For gentlemen attending a formal dinner at someone's home, you should ask if a tie is necessary, if wearing a suit is required, or if a jacket and dress pants are acceptable and appropriate. Ladies might inquire if a long dress, paired with moderate heels, is appropriate. Perhaps a blouse, jacket, and skirt would be preferred for the first meeting. You only have one chance to make a first impression, so ask questions whenever possible. In my experience, a more conservative approach can do no harm.

For informal first-time visits, jeans should not be your first option. A comfortable set of dress pants should do the trick for both ladies and gentlemen. Once again, it is better to ask than to surprise.

Always consider the weather, the event, and the dress code. Remember, go for clean and fresh and avoid any clothing that could be culturally offensive, especially for the first-time meeting.

What Type of Gifts Should You Consider When Visiting Someone's Home for the First Time?

When approaching this topic, I would look at it from the aspect of what gifts I should not consider. The idea that everyone loves receiving a gift is not entirely correct. They love receiving a gift that won't offend them. Begin with the golden rule: Assess your situation and environment. What does the person dislike? Bling or simplicity? Practical or artistic? Food or non-edible? The list can go on and on. These are normally quite straightforward, unobtrusive, and not complicated questions, but there are some cultural differences to keep in mind.

If it is a Chinese home, then do not think of gifting a clock. In Chinese, the word "clock" and the word "death" sound eerily similar, so native speakers are often reluctant to accept such gifts. In many cultures, bringing any sharp object is considered a sign of cutting off a relationship.

If you are thinking of flowers, then be careful about flower meanings in each country. Chrysanthemums are a symbol of death in Italy, and lilies and marigolds are funeral flowers in Ecuador. In India, however, marigolds are very popular as they represent the sun, symbolizing brightness and positive energy.

Italians are not joyous when receiving inexpensive or practical gifts. Their preference is for gifts of quality and style. In Turkey, on the other hand, modest gifts are welcome. Gifts with a company logo are considered poor form in France.

Unsurprisingly, a common gift is alcohol, such as nice bottle of wine as a housewarming gift, but there are reasons to be careful about this. See page 76 for more about buying alcohol as a gift.

Clearly every culture has its own specific taboo when it comes to gifts. Be sensitive of this before ignorantly stumbling into a deep dark hole of embarrassment. Consider the situation and environment as always in your etiquette equation, especially focusing on cultural background and the host's personal preferences.

Follow the Host's Cell Phone Rules as a Courtesy to Others

It is becoming more common for the host or the head of a meeting to decide a policy for cell phones at the beginning of the event. Until recently, there was even a restaurant in Vancouver, Canada that did not permit cell phones to be visible or used within the restaurant premises by guests during their time in the restaurant. Both for the convenience and purpose of not disturbing guests and for privacy, one would imagine.

We all have friends or know of people who are on their phone constantly. It can be very distracting, if not disruptive. If you are not sure if there is a phone policy, it would be very courteous of you to ask and follow the host's preference. Rules and expectations differ around the world on this topic, so always be aware of your surroundings.

In mainland China, it is not uncommon to see all the guests at one table using their cell phones simultaneously and communicating with one another via text, while seated together! They are there physically, but not entirely focused on the moment. They are enjoying the company of the other guests, taking photos, texting, and using social media live in nonstop action.

At formal occasions that I have attended, it was standard that your cell phone stay in your pocket or handbag for the duration of the evening. If you would like to enjoy a fully focused evening with guests and friends, this is not uncommon. As a host, I suggest you make an announcement at the beginning of the gathering that during dinner, please do not use phones at all. If you must, then kindly go outside and make your calls, texts, and messages.

There are many times and certain situations when phone etiquette is important. In Japan, it is extremely rude to speak loudly or use your phone on the Shinkansen, the high-speed train. If you do need to speak on your phone, you are required to leave your seat and glide away into the common area between the trains to have your discussion. In Italy, there are certain carriages that are clearly marked, "*Silenzio*, quiet carriage." On these particular carriages, there is no noise permitted for any reason whatsoever. It is a silent zone.

For formal and important gatherings, I would strongly advise against showing or using your phone, and make sure you leave it off the table. Besides, you never know what opportunities or words of wisdom you may miss from other guests if you are too preoccupied with your phone.

How to Sit Properly in the Lounge Area of Someone's Home

Being invited to someone's home is quite an honor. For those who have travelled to Asia, it is not common because homes are so small and inviting guests is almost impossible due to space restrictions. So, when you are invited, it is a huge sign of respect.

Normally, one would sit in the lounge area before or after a meal. In my experience, before sitting, I normally ask if there is a particular favorite chair that we should not sit on. It is important because it may be considered rude if we were sitting in someone's favorite chair.

If you are wearing a suit jacket and prefer to sit down wearing the jacket, follow this method. Ensure you unbutton your jacket, so no buttons are buttoned up. After unbuttoning your jacket, you may wish to pull the trousers slightly upward towards your belt with one hand on each thigh. Then you will sit down. Ensure you are sitting comfortably upright, but not too stiff like a corpse and no slouching. Place your hands stacked, one hand on your thigh and the other hand on top. Do not have them flying around like some rudderless craft in the ocean. Have a sense of presence by sitting upright, keeping your hands close to your sides, and minimizing any shifting or fidgeting.

If you are wearing a dress or skirt, your posture should be upright when seated. Keep both legs together, ensuring your undergarments and the hem of your skirt are not within sight. The same rule about jackets applies here, too. Ensure the buttons are unbuttoned. If you are wearing a skirt or dress, then use both of your hands and place them behind your body, just below the small of your back. With the palms of your hands, gracefully slide them in a downward motion so that you smooth your dress out and it is not crumpled when you sit down. This is the same motion if you are wearing pants. You should leave your feet flat on the ground, but if that is not possible, I suggest that you cross your ankles while keeping your knees together. There should be no space between your ankles.

An important point is your shoes or the soles of your feet. In certain cultures, it is an insult to show the soles of your shoes or the soles of your feet to others. Again, understand your situation and environment. This is not a concern in North America. However, in many Arab, Muslim, Hindu, and Buddhist countries, showing the sole of your shoes is an insult and can end a relationship before it even begins. Thailand, Greece, and Bulgaria are also countries in which you need to be mindful of showing the soles of shoes or feet.

There are times when there are no lounge chairs and you will sit on the floor. My advice is to watch, follow, and if you are not sure, then ask. I recall that sitting in a Japanese lounge meant sitting on the tatami floor. It was not comfortable, as I was not used to it. So if you have to, sit, grin, and bear it, even if only for a brief time.

How to Sit Properly at the Dinner Table

The dinner table is the place where millions of families make decisions. From family budgets and holiday planning to deciding which universities the children will attend and sharing daily family experiences, the dinner table is where it all happens. It is the training table where we learned how to sit correctly, hopefully.

One of the great pleasures in life is to sit down and enjoy a dinner with family and friends at the family table. It brings together this conviviality, a bonding of life itself. Also called the breaking of bread, eating together is a time to enjoy the simplest of life's pleasures, as eating with others in harmony is a gift. For Muslims, during the fasting period, the greatest respect is to be asked to break that daily fast with them. With that knowledge in mind, one should have the utmost respect, for yourself and for those amongst you with whom you are sharing the meal. You are giving yourself sustenance for the life and the breath that you take. So, act accordingly.

To sit properly, align your body in an upright position. No slouching. One's posture at the table should be straight and upright with the lower back resting slightly against the back of the chair. Do not cross your knees one over another at dinner. Keep your elbows close by your sides so as not to interfere with your neighbor while they are eating. Your wrists should be placed on the edge of the table.

Depending upon the country you are in, hands should be visible. Certainly in Italy and France, when not holding the eating utensils, your hands should be visible at all times. This goes back to the medieval times to ensure you carried no weapons. If they could see your hands always above the table, then there was no possibility of you concealing a weapon. In America, when the hands are not used for eating or drinking, they are placed upon the lap, under the table.

As for the elbows, they should not be placed on the table (page 112). The only exception is for naval dinners. Sailors who have sailed around the Cape of Good Hope, located at the base of the African continent in South Africa, or the Cape of Storms, located at the tip of the South American continent near Chile, are entitled to place one elbow on the table. If you have sailed around both Capes, you can place both elbows on the table.

Why it is Virtuous to Think Before Communicating

My late mother would tell me, "One thousand horses cannot bring back the words that have left your mouth." The meaning behind those words is think carefully before you speak. Wise words that I have adhered to and shared with my students over the years.

Beyond the spoken word, this wisdom can and should be extended to social media. You cannot really remove words or actions from the Internet once you have uploaded the text, images, or videos. The data will always be there. You must remember that we live in a world of close to 8 billion people, of which close to 5 billion people have internet access. So, it would be foolish of anyone to think that, should you say something, give an opinion, or act impulsively, that everyone will agree with you. It would be wiser to anticipate that there will be individuals and groups who disagree with you entirely. The responses can be quite vitriolic, especially given the masked identity they often cower behind. The saying the pen is mightier than the sword has extreme value to it, and one should always bear those words in mind before posting.

Diverse cultures communicate in unusual ways. The directness, emotional perspective, and formality are three aspects that can define your message and set the tone for others. These aspects ultimately cast your communication in a positive or negative light, depending upon the culture.

For example, in the United States, Germany, and the Netherlands, they tend to be more direct, while citizens in China, Japan, and India are less direct. Chinese nationals very rarely give a definitive and outright "no" as an answer. If they disagree or want to express that something cannot be done, they prefer to respond, "Let us see," "Perhaps we can review," or "We are not sure." All of these phrases say no, indirectly, whereas in North America, no means no and yes means yes.

Latin Americans are more emotionally expressive compared to Canadians and Australians. Regarding formality, North America is more likely to be casual, while most of Europe and Asia are formal. Awareness of these differences can reduce mistaken interpretations caused by innocent misunderstandings.

Whichever way you wish to communicate with others, think carefully and always be cautious, as it can reflect poorly on you. The worst part is that, in today's world with technology's breathtaking speed of dissemination, once a message has been sent, it cannot be called back, much like the words that have left your mouth.

What to Do When You Have Committed an Etiquette Faux Pas

Sound familiar? Jane greets her guest Helen with a "Thank you for coming tonight." Helen replies, "Happy to be here." Host Jane says, "I roasted a pork loin and some vegetables for dinner. Should be ready in a few minutes." Then Helen states, "Oh, I don't eat pork at all." Silence then prevails, and an uneasiness infiltrates the still atmosphere. The situation described is like darkness falling on what should have been a brilliant light for the evening. I recall a similar incident happening many years ago during my university days when friends prepared a meal for our mutual friend Ramesh. He was a Hindu and did not eat beef. They had painstakingly roasted and prepared the best beef cut for dinner. The outcome was we all went out to a restaurant to eat that night. The beef sandwiches for the next few days were heavenly though.

In the examples given, one could argue that the host and the guest have equal responsibility to inform one another. In my opinion, the onus is leaning more towards the "host" of the event. Being a host, one must consider situations that may arise and be prepared for them and also prevent any situations that might arise, by being well informed in advance of any guest restrictions or allergies.

These are two similar etiquette faux pas, but there are countless others across the world that happen daily. These are particularly minor, yet there are other faux pas that are major, and their ramifications can be serious. If you make an unintended, genuine mistake, what should you do?

If the host of the event is not being politely assertive before the event, the result is an awkward situation where the guests may not say anything if something is wrong. Equally, if you were to visit other people's homes and commit the faux pas, they may not raise any issues because they are too polite to do so. My suggestion is for you to be on the alert and aware of the atmosphere. Watch out for frowns or note if something is not being eaten or drunk. If you sense something is amiss, then ask your friend if you did anything inappropriate or if something is making them uncomfortable. If you did innocently commit a faux pas, then my suggestion would be to openly apologize, acknowledge it was unintended, and try to resolve the matter discreetly. Be gracious with your apology and accept that it is indeed an etiquette faux pas. Not everyone is well versed in the idiosyncrasies of different cultures of the world.

After such incidents, remember them and don't make the same mistake twice. One word of advice is to ask your friend to help you hold yourself accountable. Ask that if you do something wrong, they tell you immediately so that you can rectify the error and minimize any negative long-term effects on your friendship.

How to Move and Position Your Hands When Talking to Others

Italians are well known for their lively and active method of communication. When speaking, they tend to simultaneously use their hands to gesticulate up, down, and sideways. Somehow, it adds to the spice of the conversation. The fast gladiatorial thrusts of the palm or the slow motion of a ballerina are all expressive of the speaker.

During a visit to Italy, I was sitting in the presence of four fine Italian gentlemen. It was remarkable to see each individual's characteristic movements: the eyebrow frown, the lifting of shoulders, the outward thrust of the hand, and the slow double-handed sideways motion. Everyone's idiosyncratic movement illuminated their character in so many ways. This is considered normal, and quite common, in South American countries as well. The lovely animation of conversation coming alive. But this is not universal.

In Japan, when you are talking to someone, it is preferred that you restrict your hand movements to slow and deliberate motions. The gestures should not be as animated as those of Italy or South America. In fact, try to not even use your hands at all when speaking, as fast hand movements are considered somewhat threatening. The Japanese have their own method of hand movements when they speak. Certainly, when they are being spoken to, they do gesticulate. If, for example, you were to call out someone's name, let's say Aiko, she will place her index finger pointing to her face, sometimes specifically at her nose, to confirm it is her you are actually addressing.

France is like Italy: Hands are generally used when speaking to emphasize certain points. If you are going to be using your hand and you are in any Arabic countries, then you should use your right hand only, as the left hand is used for less-than-clean operations.

Make sure you give the right hand signals!

How to Avoid Challenging Discussion Topics

I remember at the time of one fine dinner that I attended, there was a particular decision made by the British government that was deemed to be quite controversial. Present at the dinner were several of my colleagues, including an Englishman. As it would happen, several of them, all from various parts of the world, started to offer their highly charged opinions about this controversial act during dinner. When they sought a response from the Englishman, he looked up, not knowing if this would escalate into a heated discussion or argument that could spoil the evening. When he replied, they were all expecting him to be defensive. Yet, in a few sentences, he disarmed the entire group. He stated, "I understand and respect what you are saying. I am not that well informed of all the facts, so I do not feel that I am able to comment. I would also like to add that I am not a representative of the British Government. It would not be for me to comment either." That was the end of that particular conversation topic, and his reply was effective in stunting any possible escalation.

Discussion at gatherings and dinners are always welcome and can positively contribute to the experience. We all know and remember such evenings. Intense arguments should be avoided at all costs. These are not the venues for controversial discussions that can begin as animated conversation then lead to openly heated argument.

How to avoid such situations? The traditional trinity of topic avoidance is money, religion, and politics. It is certainly not restricted to those topics, but they are a start. As a host of a gathering, for business or pleasure, when you see the conversation is beginning to become argumentative, I would suggest an intervention by changing the subject entirely or bringing in the next course. Always have an escape plan, should this happen, and implement it immediately. Always avoid disagreement at any functions by encouraging positive discussion amongst the group. Whenever I have a dinner party, I always have a question that I pose to the group collectively and then ask them to reply individually. It is quite amazing how different the answers are, and it opens the evening's conversation rather well, engaging those that would otherwise be rather reticent. Try it.

HOW TO EXCUSE YOURSELF FROM A CONVERSATION OR GROUP

There are a plethora of reasons as to why you would want to excuse yourself. Perhaps the conversation is as exciting as watching paint dry, or the subject is inappropriate for you. It might be as simple as wanting to go to the washroom or noticing someone arrive at the party who you want to meet. Whatever the reason, you feel compelled to leave, yet you don't wish to offend anyone.

The important thing is excuse yourself discreetly and without having to explain yourself. For example, there's no need to say, "I'm going to the washroom" or "I'm going to powder my nose." It might be more appropriate to say, "Would you excuse me for a moment?" or "I need to step away for a few minutes, but I'll be back shortly."

Timing is crucial so you don't disturb the flow of a conversation, meal, or lively interaction. The question as to when you should excuse yourself can be sensitive. It is best to do so at a particular juncture when there is a break. If you're having a seated dinner, you might want to do so in between courses. If it is a cocktail party, you might want to do so when a particular conversation has shifted away from you. At a greet and mingle, it is easier to slip away without offending anyone.

Another factor to consider is to whom you should excuse yourself. At the dinner table, the guest seated to your right certainly and the left if you prefer. Don't forget where to place your napkin when you do excuse yourself from the table (page 137)! At a cocktail party, inform the person you came with if they are present or the person standing nearest to you. At a greet and mingle, it depends on the situation, which you will need to assess.

Remember: Be considerate, leave discreetly, and always do so politely.

Communication Etiquette Regarding Cell Phones and Email

There are an estimated 6.6 billion smartphone users in the world, so the chances are you will meet many of them in your daily life. Whether it is in the office, boardroom, or on the train you took to come to work, they are there. Cell phone etiquette differs from country to country though.

In Japan, it is poor etiquette to have private conversations on your phone in the presence of others, especially strangers. If a call needs to be taken, then they step out into an area where they can take their call privately. This is so unlike North America where you can see several people talking on their phone at the same time everywhere and anywhere.

In China, don't be offended if they answer a call while they are in the middle of a meeting with you. It is not considered rude interrupting a meeting if there is a phone call. Not answering the call is considered impolite.

The pandemic has changed the rules of business engagement. Technology has allowed many people to receive business calls on their car system now while driving. So, if you are speaking to someone in the car via speakerphone, let them know immediately that they are on speakerphone and if there are other people also listening in the car. If there is anyone and if it is not convenient to take their call, then ask them to call back. If you are at the office and you want to place the call on speakerphone, then ask the other user if they mind going on speakerphone before doing so.

Most of us use email today, so understanding correct etiquette is of paramount importance. A few suggestions would be to keep your subject line pertinent and to the point. Information you send via company email should be kept on the company server and is recorded. When using a company email, you are representing the company, so you should keep your content formal, polite, and respectful, getting to the point as quickly as possible. The more you write, the greater the chances of misinterpretation, and then you have another battle to fight.

Replying promptly is professional and respectful to the person that sent you an email. Another consideration is to only CC the email to those that are involved in the business. A final word: Always check your emails before sending them out. Once you hit the send button, it is one a one-way ticket and there is no return (yet).

How to Appreciate Humor and Recognize When it is Appropriate to Share a Joke

I always admire mountaineers. They are a rather cautious but risky people because of the nature of their adventure. The enjoyment, the exhilaration, and the sense of adrenaline they experience are matchless. It's not for everyone, though. Similarly, humor is not universal, and it is not interpreted in the same way.

In certain countries, like the United States, humor has been described as slapstick and frequently quite vulgar. More often than not, the jokes are at the expense of someone or something. American classic humor differs to the modern humor, which focuses on causes and scenarios. In comparison to other styles of humor, it is different. For example, British humor figures heavily on nuances, puns, innuendo, double entendre, and wordplay. British humor leans on mocking and banter like the "roasting in good faith," and they enjoy the self-deprecation.

Everyone loves to laugh and enjoy. There are several obstacles if your company does not understand your lingua franca as you expected. Lingua franca refers to the language you are most comfortable communicating with, often referred to as your mother tongue. For example, if you grew up in a Portuguese speaking environment, then your lingua franca and mother tongue would be Portuguese. If you were to share a joke in Portuguese and others were not particularly familiar with the language or Portuguese culture, you would find the impact you expected to be deadened due to ignorance, not the lack of appreciation by the audience for your efforts. Rather than reacting with smiles and laughter at the punchline, your audience will have baffled looks and perfunctory smiles. The worst-case scenario is when misunderstandings arise, for guests who cannot understand the humor may feel insulted and then take offense.

It would be safest not to share jokes at all in unfamiliar company. Shy away from sharing jokes in a business setting or formal occasion. The safe area for jokes would be amongst very close colleagues, friends, and family who all understand the language perfectly. Once again, the golden rule is to consider the situation and environment you are in, as well as the generations with whom you are sharing humor.

DRINK
ETIQUETTE

IN THIS SECTION, you will be taken on a journey through the world of wine and spirits, learning the different and appropriate etiquette, such as how to order and taste wine, when to drink, how to drink, which glass to use and why. The romance of port and fortified wines is explained. When it comes to spirits like Cognac and whiskey, different glassware, tasting techniques, and nuances are encountered. All is revealed in this section.

You will learn the protocols for ordering wine at a restaurant and hosting a wine party. Your level of sophistication will be heightened in a very positive way, your guests will be impressed with you, and their experience will be elevated when they are with you. You will have gained a deeper appreciation for flavors and aromas and begin to develop a more discerning palate thanks to the comprehensive understanding of wine and spirits shared in this section. Above all, you get to learn more about what you do not know.

Wine Basics
DIFFERENT STYLES OF WINE

Before we investigate the complex but fascinating art of drinking wine, we must first understand the different styles of wine. Each style has its own particular set of accepted etiquette practices. There are three styles of wine: still, sparkling, and fortified.

Still wines dominate production based on volume and value globally. They are the wines that are primarily consumed from countries as far apart as Chile and China to Canada and New Zealand. An example of a still wine would be the 2014 cabernet sauvignon produced by Vinoscenti Vineyards in Surrey, British Columbia, Canada.

Sparkling wine has bubbles in it. All champagne belongs to the sparkling wine style. An example of champagne is Veuve Clicquot from France. It is important to note that not all sparkling wine is Champagne though. There's also Prosecco from Italy, for example.

Fortified wine has had alcohol added to it. The most famous examples are port and sherry. An example would be a vintage port from Taylor Fladgate, Portugal, and a fino wine from González Byass, Spain.

Why Learn the Fundamentals of Wine?

Eating out? We all do, at one time or another, with friends or family, and we often wonder about the pairing of wine and food. Is it common to think about pairing though? Absolutely it is, and with the meteoric rise of social media, the term "foodie" has become pervasive. These gastronomic professionals scour restaurants and cafés across the globe to find that unique flavor and taste. From the lofty heights of a Michelin star restaurant to the "hole in the wall" eateries, they search with a fiery intensity, carving out, discovering, and shining a light on new food and wine venues. This is a magnificent opportunity and development, as we are now exposed to even more culinary delights and adventures—with wine of course. With greater culinary choices come increased exposure to different cultures and the etiquette they follow.

Did you know there are certain wines for certain occasions? There are, in the sense there are many traditional wines to be enjoyed for certain occasions. For example, sparkling wine is more closely associated with happy occasions, celebrations, weddings, Formula One Grand Prix wins, and many other major sporting events. It can be drunk in most events and, as Napoleon said, "In victory, you deserve Champagne; in defeat, you need it." One cannot ignore passing the port to the left side of the table at the end of a meal or sipping a fine sherry before the start of a meal or while basking in the sun in southern Spain. Knowing your wines makes it easier to understand which wine to serve and the etiquette of when and how to serve the wine.

How to Taste, Select, and Pair Wine

In my experience, I have met faithful legions of wine drinkers who were either professionals in the wine industry or highly charged enthusiasts who all enjoyed wine. They appreciated the complexity of wine in terms of makeup, taste, culture, and history. The one main difference I discovered between these two camps, the professional and the enthusiast, was the inequality between the two groups when it came to tasting wine. The important procedure of how to taste wine correctly to ensure maximum benefit and to extract the aroma, nose, and palate feel was known by wine professionals and barely with enthusiasts. As an international wine judge, I happily share this knowledge so you can use this method when you enjoy your next wine tasting. By following this method, you can appreciate wine at its fullest for many years to come. You will be enlightened and shockingly surprised at the difference it makes to your enjoyment of wine and how it sharpens your sense of smell and taste.

THERE ARE THREE MAIN STEPS

The **first step** begins with the visual inspection of the glass of wine, often referred to as sight. When we look at the color of the wine, we are delving into the world of Sherlock Holmes, the great detective. We are now investigators hoping the color will offer us insight into the wine age. With more training, even more interesting facts may emerge from the color observation, like if the wine may have been produced in a cool or warm climate. It may also reveal which grape varietal may possibly have been used to make the wine. It is all a matter of deduction and thinning down the potential prospects. The visual inspection for 85% of the wine drinkers though is to ensure that there is no unwanted debris in the wine.

The **second step** is to drag out more information by nosing the aroma or bouquet of the wine. To nose the wine, we hold the wine glass by the stem in between our middle and index fingers. Then place the base of the glass on a flat surface and swirl the glass quite vigorously in a clockwise direction about eight times to allow aeration of the wine. Why eight times? I am superstitious and eight is a lucky number, so I turn it eight times. By aerating the wine, we make it easier for the aromas to be released and scented. By using this method, we can add the wonderful descriptors to the wine we have nosed.

Most important of all, you should not detect three particular aromas. They are incredibly significant and distinct: the unpleasant smell of vinegar, wet cardboard, and nail polish remover. If you do smell any of these distinct aromas, the probability of your wine being faulty is extremely high. Wine that smells of vinegar is certainly an indication of a fault known as "volatile acidity" referred to as high "VA" in the wine industry. This is often produced by bacterial activity during the wine making process or by extended exposure to air after the wine bottle has been opened. Smelling wet cardboard is a common indication of cork taint, which is a wine fault. This fault is caused by the presence of a chemical compound called 2,4,6-Trichloroanisole (TCA) present in the wine cork. Smelling nail polish remover in a wine is indicative of excess amounts of ethyl acetate in the wine. This can be caused by excessive amounts of ethyl acetate being produced during fermentation or if the wine has been exposed to excessive amounts of air. In all instances the wine has been compromised and is invariably unpleasant on the nose and palate, hence don't drink the wine and kindly ask for a replacement. Do not be discouraged that you cannot identify all the other aromas like floral, earthy, or different types of fruit. It will come, and it takes time.

The plethora and multitude of wine descriptors that you often read, see, and hear wine professionals write and talk about come after many years of experience. You can gain that skill by applying the three steps described here in your future wine adventures.

Step three is actually tasting the wine. You will take a sip the equivalent of a quarter teaspoon of wine into your mouth. Not more than that because, if you do, it will be difficult for you to aerate the wine when you suck in air through your mouth. Then you swish the wine inside you mouth, side to side, so that the mucous membranes on the inside of both your cheeks have been coated with the wine. Do this three times. Then, with your head held in a horizontal position to the ground, not looking down nor up, open your lips and create an "O" shape. Slowly suck in air for two to three seconds. Then close your mouth and swish the wine once again. Repeat this procedure twice. You can then decide to either drink the wine in your mouth or spit it out into a spit cup. You will find this technique accentuates the wine profile greatly, enhancing it and giving more clues about the wine you are tasting.

This method allows you to identify the wine through sight, nosing, and tasting. You get to appreciate the palate feel. While this process may seem quite lengthy at first, it is in fact very short, no more than forty-five seconds to a minute. That is how wine should be tasted.

This method I have shared with you is the key to greater knowledge. It will be invaluable in your wine adventure, and should you wish to learn more, please go to the Asia Pacific Wine and Spirit Institute website (www.apwasi.com) and you will be able to see the process and learn more.

Spirits Basics
DIFFERENT TYPES OF SPIRITS

In the world of hospitality, the word "spirits" is used to describe alcohol that is distilled, not fermented like wine. Spirits have a minimum of 40 percent alcohol by volume, abbreviated as ABV on bottles. Spirits can be made from a multitude of grains, like corn, rye malted barley, and even the often looked-down-upon, ignominious potato peel. Yet each of these materials will contribute towards someone's favorite tipple.

Virtually every country has its own distinctive and remarkable "spirit," which extraordinarily exudes the character of the country. Although whiskey is famously associated with Scotland, whiskey is also produced in many other countries, like Canada, Ireland, the United States, and more recently India. There is "raki" from Turkey, "ouzo" from Greece, and "grappa" from Italy. China has its own very powerful "Moutai," and Mexico has "tequila." There are countless others, too numerous to mention. The important factor is that spirits are traditionally sold with a 40 percent ABV, but it can be higher. I have seen spirits as high as 70 percent ABV.

How to Taste Spirits

There is a major difference in how you taste spirits compared to wine. With most spirits, one is charmed by the alluring copper and golden amber appearance. Yet, the color of spirits does not reveal inner secrets as the color of wine does. We want to know about where it's from and how it was made. We want the "spirits" to confess their heritage to us. So how do we taste spirits? Once again, like in wine tasting, there are three steps in spirit tasting.

Step one is the visual aspect of eyeing the spirit. It does have its value more in esoteric terms of color. Compared to wine revelations, spirits are less informative. Spirits are distilled and the final liquid is clear. In many instances, coloring is added to the final product. Scotch, for example, has E150a, known as "spirit coloring," added to it. There are relative influences that come from the barrel, and to some degree the aging, but it is not as impactful as the coloring that is added.

The **second step** is the nosing. On the nose, one should not swirl the spirit as one would with wine. This would merely agitate the elevated level of ABV, so all you would smell would be pure alcohol, which would temporarily deaden your sense of smell. Rather, let the alcohol sit calmly in your glass after it has been poured out. Allow it to settle, then pick up the glass in one hand and nose it a few times. Then, try a second nosing method that opens up the spirit. Start by picking up the glass in one hand and using the other hand to cover the top of the glass. Hold the glass close to your body to allow some of your body heat to warm it while keeping the glass top covered. Hold it for a few minutes until you see condensation forming within the glass. When this happens, gently remove the glass from your body. Visualize the condensation by bringing the glass up to eye level. Then remove the hand covering the top of the glass and bring the glass to your nose. The aroma and the intensity will be quite different from the first method of nosing.

The **third step** is tasting the spirit. Unlike in wine, we do not swirl the spirit in our mouth, as that would coat the mucous membrane inside our cheeks, numbing it with 40 percent (or more) ABV. This would obliterate our ability to taste anything of value. To appreciate spirit tastings significantly, my suggestion is to take about a sixth of a teaspoon equivalent of spirit into your mouth. Place the liquid in the middle of your tongue and then begin a chewing motion, as if you are chewing a piece of steak. Keep on "chewing" until you notice that there is an accumulation of saliva in your mouth. Only then can you swallow the spirit. You will notice a kaleidoscope of flavors and sensations within your mouth.

How to Select Spirits with Company

How you choose spirits with company can vary greatly. Once again, we must rely on the golden rule of understanding your situation and the environment. If you are visiting a country, it can be a great treasure and adventure to try spirits from that country you are visiting. If you are having a guest in your country, you might want to suggest trying a spirit from your country. Which spirit you choose will depend on whom you are enjoying the spirit with.

How to Pair Spirits with Food

It is my belief that the best person to decide what will pair well with your favorite spirit is you. But having said that, one should not ignore the experience and advice of others. There are traditional pairings, like Scotch and duck breast, brandies and dark chocolate, rye with Japanese sashimi or sushi, and tequila with tacos. The combinations are as limitless as there are stars in the heavens. Not every pairing will suit everyone. So, my suggestion is going out, exploring possibilities, and seeing what works well for you.

Wine, Spirits, and Etiquette

By exploring the basics in the beginning of this chapter, you've been introduced to the fundamentals of how to enjoy wine and spirits. Far too often, many people freeze and develop a gentle sweat when asked at a business dinner or gathering to suggest a wine or spirit for the group. Then, of course, you must nose and taste the wine before giving your approval. This rest of this chapter should diminish any inner fears you may have had and set you on a more confident path. More importantly, your foundation is now firmly set so we can build up from this foundation with the etiquette of wine and spirit application.

HOST ETIQUETTE CONSIDERATIONS FOR ORDERING WINE AT A RESTAURANT

If you are hosting lunch or dinner at a restaurant, you might like to order some wine. Before taking charge and ordering wine at the table, it would be gracious of you to ask if any of the guests would like to select the wine. In most instances, they tend to shy away, but if there is a guest who would like to order wine, then allow them to do so. When I am at dinner with guests, they always ask me to select the wine for dinner and I agree with a smile. If your guests prefer not to risk selecting a poor wine because of ignorance, then you as the host will take up the challenge.

It would be extremely sensible to ask your guests if they would like to join you in sharing a bottle of wine. If not many people would like to join you, then you should decide if you still wish to order a bottle or not. You could also give your guests another option if the bottle seems like too much.

It might be easier or preferred to order wine by the glass. Your guests have different palates and preferences, so it is easier for them to pair their meal with individual wine choices. If this is the case, then be gracious and allow them to order as they please.

If different meals are being ordered, you could have a hybrid situation, depending upon your generosity. Those who wish to order a glass of wine can do so, and those who wish to share a bottle with you can do so as well. Remember, you are the host, and they are your guests.

If it is a set meal, your responsibilities of selection as a host are simplified significantly. For example, a roast beef would be significantly elevated by pairing it with a red wine. Seafood and chicken both pair remarkably well with white wine or perhaps even a rosé.

What to Do When a Guest Does Not Drink Alcohol

Never force a drink on anyone who does not consume alcohol. Perhaps a guest does not want to drink because they are not of a legal age yet. To drink, one must always be cognizant of the legal age for enjoying either wine or spirits. Adherence to the laws of the country where you are drinking is non-negotiable, and be aware that the age of legality is different from country to country. For example, in Canada the legal drinking age is 19, in the United States it is 21, and in Cuba 16-year-olds can drink. So, you must be aware once again of your situation and environment.

For whatever reason they choose not to drink, be it age, personal preference, religious beliefs, or alcohol rehabilitation, respect their choice and move along. As the host, when one of your guests does not drink alcohol, there must be no pressure exerted. There is no need to coerce or force your guest to drink any wine or spirit. You should rather offer them alternatives, perhaps a fruit drink, a virgin cocktail, water, tea, or coffee.

Over the decades I have been at many events where there are teetotalers and those who drink having a wonderful evening together. You can have an enjoyable event without having to drink alcohol; billions of people do it across the globe everyday. Never force people—it's not polite. The rudeness will escalate if you keep on pestering them and making it an issue.

If you wish to be even more courteous, you may even ask them if they mind you enjoying the glass of wine or spirit in front of them. This would be highly respectful, as they may feel that even being in the presence of alcohol is offensive to them. To avoid any issues, it is proper etiquette to respect guests and their beliefs.

How to Select and Order Wine at the Host's Request

Selecting wine for dinner, especially when there are several guests present, can be quite daunting. Having read the section in this book about wines, you should feel less trepidation and greatly encouraged to take the task at hand with full enthusiasm. Thank your host for this honor, and then ask the host and other guests at the table if there are any preferences for wine from a specific country or made from a particular variety of grape. If there are no suggestions, then feel free to select the wine with no pre-set limits.

Even though the host has asked you to select the wine, be modest in your choice regarding cost, unless you know that cost is not a consideration for the host. To avoid embarrassing the host regarding the cost of the wine, select a medium-priced wine and a slightly more expensive alternative one for the host to consider. Then, pass the wine list back to the host and let him know your two choices, stating that both are equally superb. Allow the host the final choice. If the response is that you should decide, then you have the blessing for the higher priced wine selected. If the response is that the host prefers the less expensive wine, then you are assured that your wine selection will not break the bank. The host may request to see both bottles, in which case you can order both bottles for an examination.

Once your selection is made, request that the two selections you had in mind initially be brought to you. This allows a final possible change of heart for the host if they so wish. When the bottles are brought to the table, you can let the host and guests see the wine bottles. Then make the final decision. Upon the wine selection, you will then be asked to taste the wine (page 68). Enjoy the wine!

As a backup plan, if you really are not confident and in doubt, you can always ask the restaurant wine professional to assist you in selecting a bottle of wine.

Considerations When Ordering Wine Amongst Friends or Guests

When you are in charge of ordering the wine, there are three main factors to consider. The **first factor** is type of food being ordered. Is everyone eating the same meal from a set menu? Or are they ordering different meals? Since it is best to pair the wine with the meal (page 60), this is an important consideration. If everyone is eating from a set meal, then you could certainly order by the bottle. When there are many different meals, allowing guests to order by the glass may be best.

The **second factor** is the sophistication of the group. If the other guests enjoy wine but are not aficionados like yourself, you could be forgiven for ordering a simple but palatable wine. Respectfully, their palate may not be as sophisticated as yours, and sharing an expensive wine does not necessarily mean that they will enjoy it. On many an occasion, I have witnessed expensive wine being ordered with the best intentions that guests are treated to a truly fine wine, only for the guests to be dissatisfied and the wine to be unappreciated and wasted.

A **third factor** is the cost. How much are you prepared to pay for a bottle of wine? Remember, you may have to order more than one bottle if the group is rather boisterous and enjoys wine tremendously. It may also be necessary to order both a white and red wine if the meals ordered by the group justify the dual order.

Understanding and applying the combination of all three factors will hold you in good stead with your wine selection approach.

How to Introduce a Bottle of Wine to Dining Guests

There's often the awkward silence that accompanies a dinner party where the guests are slowly getting a sense of each other. It is a gentle social minefield. I have found that when I introduce a bottle of wine, the entire scenario changes. The reason is that the wine initiates so many conversational topics.

The wine you order is evidence of what happened in the year that the wine was produced. It reflects what happened in that particular year, in that particular country and region. Every wine made has a story, as we each have our personal stories, whether individually or collectively. From an incredibly early age, we all loved stories, so beginning with a story is a good place to start conversations.

I would impress upon you that when you are introducing a bottle of wine, take a few moments to understand the wine that you are going to share with your guests. Consider where it was made, the country where it was produced. There is always a uniqueness of the region, as well as the climate, soil, and other unique aspects to consider. People often enjoy knowing the historical background of a winery, who made it, and the vintage. How does it compare to the best and the worst from that region? If you are not sure how to prepare yourself for such topics, then know that you can find most of this information on the wine label.

There is so much that you can glean from a label. Every bottle must have, by law, the name of the winery and country where it was produced, the predominant grape used to make the wine, the vintage year, and the alcohol by volume. If you would like to be more precise, at the touch of your fingertips you can discover more about that wine using the Internet.

Just a simple bottle of wine is the catalyst that can break down the walls of silence at any social gathering.

How to Taste the Wine When it Arrives at your Table

There are three steps to tasting a bottle of wine: sighting, nosing, and tasting (page 61). If you have been given the privilege and honor of tasting the wine, then do so with the confidence, reflection, and seriousness that it demands. Why, you ask? Is this not a perfunctory movement? It is not! So many people that I have met have shared with me how many wines, literally hundreds of thousands, that they have tried. Yet, they are missing the fine-tuned technique to decipher the wonderous wine code. There is an advantage to formal wine training; it offers the code-breaking method you need.

In most cases, whether it is music, art, or education, undertaking a formal program has advantages. That is not to say that those that don't have that formal education are any less capable. When you have formal training, the fulfilment level of understanding of that subject is quite different, as you are taught what to observe, what it means, and how to evaluate objectively. This certainly is true when it comes to wine tasting.

Imagine that you have ordered the wine, and the sommelier, or the wine steward, has brought the wine to you. They will repeat the name of the wine to you to ensure it is the one you ordered. You should either nod or say yes and thank you. They will then open the bottle of wine and pour you a short pour of 1 ounce and hand you the glass of wine to taste and inspect it to see if it is acceptable or not. They might also give you the cork to smell and observe. If they do, pick up the cork and inspect it. Look for cracks that indicate the wine was not kept under optimum condition and also smell the cork for any unpleasantness. This is all part of the wine etiquette. You will then follow the three steps of wine tasting (page 61).

Correct Etiquette for Tasting Champagne and Sparkling Wine

The only difference between sparkling wines and still wines is the bubbles, and that is enough to warrant some changes to the tasting etiquette for sparkling wines. Consider the three-step process for wine tasting: the sighting, nosing, and tasting (page 61). Fortunately, the first step, sighting, is the same for both sparkling and still wine.

In the second step, the nosing, you do not swirl the sparkling wine as you would a still wine. If you do, you will prematurely end the magical show of the bubbles that are gently and consistently rising to the top of the glass. Other than that change, the rest remains the same for nosing sparkling wine. Follow the same observations and identify aromas.

The difference with the third step is that you must be cognizant of the explosion of bubbles in your mouth when you taste sparkling wine. We call this explosion of bubbles the mousse of the sparkling wine. The etiquette for tasting sparkling wine demands you inspect that there are indeed bubbles still present in addition to the other steps for wine. The effervescence, the bubbles that make their delightful journey from the base of the flute to the top of the glass, is quite magical, captivating, and extremely attractive. There are so many different sparkling wines around the world, such as the famous Prosecco from Italy, Cava from Spain, cap classique from South Africa, sekt from Germany, and of course, Champagne from France. Take your time to enjoy tasting a variety of them.

SELECTING THE APPROPRIATE GLASS FOR SPARKLING WINE

There are three main options for sparkling wine glasses: the flute, the coupe, or the tulip glass. Whichever glass you choose, do not accept mediocre glasses. Always treat yourself as you should, with the highest level of comfort.

The flute is my personal preference. When drinking sparkling wine, I go for the long, narrow, slender looking flute wine glass. The tall, statuesque shape of the glass accentuates the bubbles, and the height of the glass permits the bubbles to be visually captured at their best as they gently, slowly, and elegantly rise. Additionally, the shape of the glass allows you to absorb and nose the autolytic aromas that go hand in hand with Champagne. This glass is perfect for Cava, Prosecco and crémant.

Another option is the coupe. The shape of the coupe was allegedly made by making a mold from one of Marie Antoinette's breasts. The size and the shape of champagne coupes used this mold for centuries until recently. The coupe glass gives more of a burst to the nose and a fuller taste on the palate because of the wider opening. Coupe glasses are more popular in cruise ships and at weddings. The Champagne Mountain, a 10 to 15 tier high pyramid built from glasses, is big for such events, and it is easier to build such a high structure with coupes than flutes.

The tulip glass is a variation of the flute. The main difference is that the tulip tends to bulge out more in the middle of the glass, while the flute is slender. This glass is ideal for Champagne, since the height is tall enough to enjoy the bubbles and to let the aromas develop as they make the journey to the top of the glass.

What to Do When the Wine Ordered is Faulty

There is a difference between a faulty wine and a wine that you may not like personally. It is important to differentiate this because, if you don't like the wine you selected, it does not mean that it is faulty. Likewise, you may enjoy a wine, but it is faulty. A late vintage pinot noir is often mistaken for faulty. Pinot noir is well known for this, as the wine tends to have a robust and off-putting aroma if it is an old vintage. It is an acquired aroma and taste but not faulty.

So, how do we define wine as faulty? That would be a wine that has very strong, pronounced notes of vinegar and has changed significantly. Wet cardboard notes and nail polish remover are also indicators that the wine has a very good chance, if not a certainty, of being faulty.

Should you be in the unfortunate situation of having ordered a faulty wine, take the appropriate steps to change the wine in a calm, refined, and patient manner. Discreetly and calmly call for the sommelier to come to your table. If they are at your table already, then inform them by whispering in his ear what you have discovered and ask him if he would kindly change it. In many instances, the restaurants will do so without question. They may ask you if you would like a replacement bottle or to select new wine. I would advise selecting a different wine altogether, as a replacement bottle may be from the same case.

Now, there may be an instance when the wine you selected is very old, perhaps 20 years plus. In this case, the sommelier may say to you that they cannot guarantee the quality of this wine due to the age. If you decide to select the wine anyway and it is faulty, you will likely still be charged for it, but at a lesser fee. It is recommended that you learn the return policy for faulty wine at the establishment before ordering the wine. Under no circumstances are you to make a scene.

When is it Appropriate to Return Restaurant Wine After the Initial Tasting?

As has been mentioned, there are three aspects of a faulty wine. They are vinegar, wet cardboard, and nail polish remover aromas. Should you identify any of these during your initial nosing, they all qualify as faulty. It is then quite right for you to kindly ask the sommelier to replace it or offer you the opportunity to change your selection of wine.

However, if you do not smell any of those three unpleasant aromas, yet you do not like the wine itself because of the flavor, that is a different matter. That does not give you the right to return the wine.

Technically, the wine is perfect. The problem is that you do not personally like the taste. That is an entirely different matter, and it is poor etiquette to force this matter ahead. If you really don't like the wine, you can let the sommelier know. In some fine dining restaurants, they may replace it for you knowing that the reason is personal taste, not the wine itself.

Should this happen when you are settling the final bill, your tip should reflect the sommelier's generosity, as per proper etiquette and as a way to show your appreciation. The amount of the tip will depend on the prevailing tipping culture, which will differ depending on the situation and environment you are in. If you were in America where tipping is expected, you might offer anywhere from 15–20 percent, and in Japan where tipping is frowned upon, then a zero percent tip would not be considered rude.

How to Decant a Wine at Home

Learning how to decant wine is good etiquette, as it shows your respect toward your guests, and you owe it to yourself to fully appreciate the wine to be tasted. There are three main methods to either aerating or decanting wine.

The **first method** is the decanter. Decanters are a necessary and vital piece of equipment that you should have in your personal arsenal of wine equipment. The wine is slowly and deliberately poured into a glass container that has a large surface area. This allows rather young wine to interact with more oxygen in the air to smooth out roughness on the palate feel. Red wines, if young, will do well if decantated an hour before serving. The rule is the older the wine, the shorter the decanting period, and the younger the wine, the longer the period. I like to decant the wine when the guests are there, and it can be an activity and topic of discussion to break the ice with guests.

Young red wines, like young Bordeaux, Australian shiraz, and even red Napa Valley wines, benefit from this exercise. Interestingly enough, one of the main reasons wine drinkers prefer to decant their wine is that the owner of the bottle is unable to restrain their excitement and wants to try the wine now, rather than wait a few years. Wines that are heavily tannic and young vintages should be decanted.

The **second method** is the aerator. This is less impressive than the decanter method, as it is usually connected to the wine bottle and can be described as the "hurried" method of decanting. This method can be applied universally to all types of red and white wines, although I would prefer the decanting method for high-quality red wines.

The **third method**, known as hyper decanting, is not practiced often. One would pour the wine into a blender and literally give it a whirl. This method maximizes the exposure of wine to the oxygen in the harshest possible manner but in the shortest time. If you plan to use this method, I would not recommend it for any wines of quality. This method leans more towards wines of mediocre, questionable or lower quality.

It is good form to know which one to use with which wine.

When Should You Decant Wine?

Wines are fickle, like humans. They vary from vintage to vintage and succumb to the charms of the weather, be it good or severely bad. They protest loudly when the grapes have low sugar levels and lack structural characteristics needed to produce a delicious wine in poor weather. In good weather, grapes flourish like the summer sun or a mother gleaming and smiling at her new cooing baby, and superb wine is made most of the time.

Depending on the weather and vintage, decanting the wine is not always a required step before serving wine. In general, broad strokes, should the wine belong to the overly used descriptor of "big, bad, and bold" category of a red wine, like sagrantino, cabernet sauvignon, barolo made from nebbiolo, syrah, amarone made from corvina, molinara, and rondinella grapes, one should decant. The reason is that these wines, when young, express a strong muscular structure and tight grippy aspects of tannins. The fruit is not yet fully released, but it will be in time. With less than four to five years on the vintage chronometer, opening a high-quality wine from any of the aforementioned grapes could be considered a sacrifice of indulging now and forgoing a real pleasure for the years ahead.

In vintage age terms, four to five years for these wines is considered very young, especially when you understand that these wines only start to bloom and peak after ten years from their vintage and get supremely better as they get older. Mind you, I need to be clear that this applies to top-quality wines predominantly. For example, a Grand Cru Left Bank Bordeaux cabernet sauvignon will be blatantly different from an Argentinian cabernet sauvignon. You might be forgiven for wanting to decant these top-quality wines as soon as you arrive home. It's very tempting, and I know many people who buy a case and decant one bottle to taste it. The rest they leave in their cellars, allowing the magic of time to elevate the stature of the wine.

So, when you make the decision to decant, there are several considerations. Deliberate on the age of the wine, as this will determine length of the decanting time. The younger the wine, the longer you should leave the wine to mellow. It can be up to two hours or more. This allows the wine to interact with the oxygen in the air, making the aggressive tannins more supple and softer, supporting the fruit notes and expressions of flavor on the nose to enhance the palate experience. When your tannins are supple and soft, the wine is not so bitter and astringent.

Should you decant an older wine, twenty to forty years old, the mellowing time is tightly reined in to perhaps a few minutes as opposed to hours. Remember, the older wine has not been exposed to air for over twenty years at least, so when it is exposed, it begins to break down immediately. Unnecessarily long exposure can cause the wine to become undrinkable in a short space of time.

Having said that, I enjoyed a 1968 red from Portugal recently that I had decanted for about 3 minutes. It was stunning, beyond expectations, and one for the memory banks. Every wine is different, and that's the part of wine that is so exciting. It offers a plethora of unexpected outcomes. Wondering how knowing when to decant a wine relates to etiquette? Understanding which wines age well and when gives you the opportunity to share this great understanding of wine with your guest. Expressing that knowledge by sharing wine at its best is etiquette towards your guest.

Wine Tasting Etiquette at a Winery

When visiting wine country, whether it is in Bordeaux in France, Valpolicella in Italy, Ningxia in China, or Mendoza in Argentina, the wine tasting etiquette rules remain unchanged. Far too often I have witnessed individuals blocking others from getting their glasses filled with wine, not deliberately but unknowingly. Sadly, I have seen guests drinking their flights of wine in a way that obliterates their taste buds and experience. All of this could be prevented by simply following wine-tasting etiquette.

All wineries have a tasting room, and etiquette should be adhered to and followed there for everyone's benefit. When you enter a tasting room at a winery, it's best to ask them what flights they have and what their flagship wine is. They will be happy to suggest certain wines for you. Once your decision has been made, you will be poured a wine flight, which is three or more wines.

In terms of etiquette, and for your enhanced pleasure, there is a specific order that you should enjoy tasting this flight of wine. The rule is to start with glasses from your left side, then move to the right. Taste young wines then old wines, then white to red, light bodied to full bodied, and dry to sweet.

Another suggestion for when you taste the wines in the flight: Don't immediately finish the last sip of every single glass. At your initial tasting, leave perhaps a third of the initial pour of the wine. This enables you to go back and notice, observe, and smell the wine later and notice any differences from the initial taste to the later one. Wines do change after several minutes in a glass. Make a point of noticing this and follow the new tasting etiquette. It makes a difference to your tasting experience.

Wine Tasting Etiquette at a Wine Festival

Wine festivals often remind me of music concerts where there is a constant jostling, gyrating, elbowing, and flaying of hands in the air, as everybody wants to quickly get their quota of enjoyment. In wine festivals, it's not their pound of flesh but their ounces of wine they want.

I must differentiate between trade tastings, which most wine festivals have for the importers and the commercial buyers, and public tastings. There is a clear distinction between public tastings and trade tastings. Ask any of the wine staff or professionals who pour at such events, and they will have remarkable stories to share of drunk patrons who attended public tastings. Public tastings have a distinctly different atmosphere, circus-like really, and when it is a trade tasting, the difference is startling.

When wine festivals are opened up to the general public, it is common for members of the industry to fear those moments. When the hordes descend, the public has one objective, and that is to literally try and consume as much wine in as short a space of time possible. It can be rather brutal on the sensitivities of the pourers behind the table, yet they are subjected to this continual assault for hours. They have to be pleasant and courteous, so the least we can do is assist them.

The correct etiquette when approaching the table where the wine is being poured is to have your own wine glass at the ready. The pourer will pour some wine into your glass when you stretch your arm out towards him, with a smile of course. After receiving the wine, step aside to allow other guests the chance to enjoy the wine that is being offered at the table. By stepping aside, you are creating a space for the person behind you to come forward. If you stand at the table, not moving after you have received your pour, all you are doing is blocking that table from sharing their wine with others at the festival. This creates a backlog, as the people behind you have to wait until you leave.

Wondering which of the hundreds of stations to start with? My suggestion when choosing stations would be to always move through tables from whites to reds, light body to full body, and dry to sweet when possible. This next piece of advice may seem contrary to your enjoyment, but believe me, after tasting eighteen to twenty-four different wines or after visiting seven or eight pouring stations, it is very easy to become inebriated if you don't spit. Always use a spit cup or the spittoon that may be provided. Also, if during the course of the festival you have a moment, have a quick bite so that you are not tasting wine on an empty stomach.

Armed with this knowledge, I am sure you will be more perceptive to your surroundings and create a steady flow.

How to Select a Bottle of Wine as a Gift

The golden rule of remembering the situation and environment is of paramount importance here. Several questions need to be answered to establish if giving a bottle of wine as a gift is suitable or not. Whenever you are giving a gift, it is important that the person receiving it appreciates your thoughts and efforts that went into selecting the gift for them.

It may sound simple enough, but start by asking yourself if your friend drinks wine or not. If not, then choose another gift. If the answer is yes, then you extend your thoughts to wondering if they are a casual drinker or a collector. That would give you an idea of the type, quality, and cost of the wine you should buy.

Another question to consider is if they are permitted to accept bottles of wine. There may be a reason they may not be allowed to accept such a gift. Also think about the purpose of gifting the bottle of wine. Is it a special occasion for the person who is receiving the gift? Are they a collector of wine, or is this just a bottle of wine that you're going to enjoy with them? If you wish to drink the bottle with them as part of the gifting experience, let the recipient know. If you prefer that they place the bottle in their cellar as part of their collection, also let them know. Feeling generous? Buy two identical bottles: one for sharing and one for the cellar.

I cannot impress enough the importance of understanding the situation before gifting bottles of wine. There are even times when you should be subtle, such as when choosing an expensive wine. Would the recipient feel embarrassment when gifted the most expensive wine, perhaps seeing it as overkill in terms of the pricing and quality of the wine? That may sound peculiar to you, as who would not want to receive an expensive bottle of wine? To be truthful, the answer is many people might feel uncomfortable, especially if they are not able afford such generosity in return. Also, the expensive bottle of wine does not automatically translate into enjoyment for the recipient. Personally, they may enjoy a less expensive wine if it suits their palate better. It would be better to gift based on their taste than the expense of the wine.

To summarize, consider the price, the reason, and the objective of giving that bottle of wine.

Selecting the Appropriate Glass for Whiskey

Glasses do make a difference. From a personal point of view, the cut, gleam, and shimmering light on the liquid as it sits in the glass makes the enjoyment of that tipple and experience even more appealing and memorable. There are five variations that one could use for whiskey: the Glencairn, copita, highball, snifter, or tumbler.

Let's begin with the very famous Glencairn whiskey glass, which is quite robust. It is short with a solid base and thicker glass, which I suspect is for easier holding. This is a perfect glass for swirling, and the glass has a bowl shape near the base that allows the aromas to open. The tapered mouth of the glass allows one to truly smell the nuances the whiskey has to offer.

The tulip-shaped glass, also known as the copita style, is a small glass ideal for sherry that is also used for whiskey tasting. It has a narrow rim, and the bowl is narrow and quite tall considering the size of the glass. This all adds and concentrates the aromas. The glass is easily held in one hand if one wishes to warm up the spirit like a single malt.

If you are using the whiskey as a cocktail, then you should use a highball glass. This is extremely popular in Japan. This glass is a tall and slim tumbler whose size enables ice and a large non-alcoholic mixer to be added to the whiskey.

The ubiquitous snifter glass, which has a closer association to Cognac, is now also used to enjoy drinking whiskey. The glass has a very generous, wide body. However, the rim is overly broad, and it is designed in a manner that, even when it is held at an angle, the spirits will not spill out. The wideness of the glass allows the strong, pungent aromas to be released, leaving behind the more subtle and welcomed notes.

The classic whiskey tumbler, clean in appearance or with crystal patterns, has a broad rim. It is ideal for cocktails. The wide rim might make the purist hope to engage in every aroma from the spirit, but the wide rim is not good for that. A tumbler is best left to cocktails.

First determine how you prefer your whiskey, then choose the style of whiskey glass that best matches that preference. May your glass be full.

The Nuances of Brandy and Cognac

When you cross the river Charente in the Cognac region of France and you are greeted with aging warehouses that house Cognac from the 1800s, you realize Cognac is steeped with history. With that pedigree, it is almost unimaginable not to have etiquette and Cognac mentioned in the same breath.

Cognac, the drink, comes from the region of Cognac located to the north of Bordeaux in Southwest France. There, Cognac is made with several different quality levels, which range from the entry level of VSOP (Very Superior Old Pale) to the midrange VS (Very Special) and the more aged Cognac called XO (Extra Old). Cognac is a brandy, but not all brandy is Cognac. Sound familiar? It should, as it has the same pattern as sparkling wine and Champagne. Cognac is made from the grape ugni blanc. This grape originated in Italy where it is called trebbiano. Cognac, as mentioned before, is really a brandy, but for marketing and protection of the region, only brandy produced from the region of Cognac can be named as Cognac. While not all brandy is Cognac, there is wonderful brandy made all over the world. There is Spanish brandy, French brandy not made in Cognac like Armagnac, and brandy from South Africa and Chile.

The optimal drinking glass for Cognac is the snifter glass. This glass allows you to hold the glass very easily and comfortably in the palm of your hand. It is easy to swirl the amber liquid and enjoy the slow descent of the fluid down the side of the glass. Another advantage of using the snifter glass is that you can hold the glass at an angle that is not horizontal, and because of the breadth and depth of the glass, the Cognac will not spill out. Equally, the broad base and the narrow room retains the flavor profile. With the most suitable pairing of a cigar, one may have the setting for a perfect evening.

Spirit Tasting Etiquette at a Distillery

One should always remember consideration of other guests when at any tastings. It could be a long-awaited rum distillery tasting, a whiskey tasting in Scotland, or even a bourbon tasting in Kentucky. Etiquette is first and foremost on the mind. Etiquette at a distillery is not dissimilar to the etiquette that you would display at a winery. The only difference is, as mentioned in the introduction to this chapter, how you taste spirits as opposed to wine (page 63).

There are many pearls of wisdom that your guide will share with you during your tour and tasting. Take full advantage of their knowledge and even ask them about local etiquette concerning certain spirits—it's quite fascinating. It's my suggestion that your tasting should comprise no more than four spirits, with the absolute maximum of five, at any one sitting. Spirits have an extremely high level of 40% or more ABV. It will be an assault on your senses and numb them into oblivion should you be drinking more, and you will no longer appreciate what you are tasting. If you are planning to visit distilleries, two a day in my experience sums it all up rather well.

As a final suggestion, it's always good to have water on the side. Follow the spirit tasting procedures that have been outlined (page 63), and I wish you a great tasting wherever you may be.

When to Drink Spirits While Dining

Many of you might say, you can drink wine before, during, and after food. Not totally unreasonable on the surface, and who can argue with antiquity when the Greeks and Romans gave it their blessing. The Greeks would drink after their meals, while the Romans would drink during their meals, and Americans initiated drinking before the meal. When it comes to spirits though, is it really consumed before the main meal? It really depends on where you are drinking spirits, as it can be with the meal and before.

In Mexico, they drink tequila before the meal, as they believe it boosts your metabolism, and also after dinner, as it aids digestion. In China, Moutai, the national drink made from sorghum and organic wheat, primarily is enjoyed during the meal. The rules of etiquette there are never drink before making a toast or being toasted, do not stop drinking before the host does, and always empty your glass. Oh, and don't forget to hold the glass in your right hand!

Prevailing etiquette is that before meals, spirits can be consumed in the form of aperitifs, as they stimulate the appetite. Many aperitifs are made from gin, vodka, and tequila. It's not common to have hard spirits, like Cognac or whiskey, during the meal. These two spirits are served after the meal, in fact after dessert. Rum, especially dark aged rum, is popular as an after-meals drink.

A formal evening might begin with an aperitif or sparkling wine, then move on to a wine during the meal. Depending on the number of courses, it is not uncommon to enjoy four to five different wines. Dessert is served with a sweet wine and ends with cheese and port. After that, the whiskey and Cognac are shown and shared with huge pride by the host. At this time, cigars are also brought out in their splendor to match the spirits available.

What to Do When You Do Not Like the Spirit You Ordered at a Bar

It has been my experience that at most international city bars, it would not be considered poor etiquette if you were to ask the barman to pour you a taster of the spirit that you would like to enjoy. In fact, they are quite enthusiastic when they see someone wanting to explore and broaden their horizons. This is their realm, and they have the opportunity to showcase their knowledge and share a story or two with you at the same time.

I would try and ask the barman if they wouldn't mind letting you try, as the Scots would say, "a wee dram," which is about an eighth of a fluid ounce. If there are no spirits that you like, be kind and gracious enough to the barman to offer a tip for their troubles. The pours that they give you will be less than an ounce, so it is not a difficult request for them to accommodate you.

However, if you did not follow this process and ordered a drink that you really do not like, in most establishments, they may not charge you for it. They might be open to changing the drink for you if you tell them immediately after tasting the drink. However, if they inform you that you will be charged, then pay for the drink. At the end of the day, it was your choice and your decision.

Scanning the bar for a different spirit is quite an experience; it certainly was for me in Scotland.

Port Traditions and Faux Pas

Port comes from Portugal. This wonderful, fortified drink rose to prominence between 1805 and 1810 and has since held its position as a truly masterful wine that has been tasted, admired, and revered by kings and emperors. Port is made by adding alcohol to the wine "must," halting the continued fermentation of the wine and resulting in the sweet style and high alcohol content it has. Thus it is called fortified wine.

There are two main styles of port—tawny and red. Tawny port is aged in barrels for many years and has an oxidative characteristic. Literally, the older the better. Red port is bottled once it is made. There are several different levels of red port. The entry level is ruby, reserve ruby, and Late Bottled Vintage (LBV) port, which can be filtered or unfiltered. Of course, Vintage Port (VP) is the most highly sought-after red port. VP is considered the best red port made, and it is generally agreed that in each decade, only two vintages are considered worthy and suitable and named as Vintage Port.

Set amongst the backdrop of the romance of the seas and the naval tradition, port, by name, conjures up adventure. Port aficionados have even created, through the ages, drinking traditions. One of the most famous involves the phrase, "Do you know the Bishop of Norwich?" This tradition revolves around the way port is shared. Once the port has been decanted, it is initially held by the host who will pour for his guest to the right of him and then for himself. Next, he will pass the port to his left, and that guest will pour themselves some port. This will continue around the table, keeping the port decanter moving only in a clockwise direction. The port bottle is never passed to your right-hand side and is never passed across the table. When the conversation is very agreeable or too much port has been drunk and guests become sleepy, sometimes the port decanter does not get passed. To make light of an awkward and impolite situation around the person responsible for the holdup, the tradition is to ask, "Do you know the Bishop of Norwich?" The sublime message here would clearly be, "Please pass the port onward."

The Bishop of Norwich is attributed to Henry Bathurst, who was the Bishop of Norwich from 1805 to 1837. The bishop tended to fall asleep at the table toward the end of a meal, so he frequently did not pass the port.

So next time you hear the phrase, it is a gentle reminder to please pass the port to your left and follow etiquette.

Methodology to Enjoying Spirits and Wine

Is there a set order to how you enjoy spirits and wine at a meal? There are those that argue unquestionably yes, and those that would say definitively no. It really depends on you.

From a personal perspective, whenever I hold or have attended sumptuous formal dinners, they always begin with a sparkling wine. This sets the mood and can be paired with a selection of hors d'oeuvres if not yet seated. If seated, then the sparkling wine is often paired with a light salad.

Once that has been served, there is normally a small amount of spirit poured, perhaps one and a half ounces. That is used for the first toast of the evening, usually to celebrate a particular event, service, or person. Thereafter, we have a white wine with seafood, followed with a rosé wine paired with a white meat.

The next course of lamb or steak goes exceptionally well with either a barolo, amarone, or a Grand Cru Classé from Bordeaux. Without exception, the wine would have to be a big, boisterous, highly structured red wine that would match the weight and bountiful flavor of the meat.

After the meal, there would be dessert, and the accompanying wine would be a chilled noble rot wine, like Sauternes. For those less inclined for the sweet wines, a late harvest could be selected. A personal favorite of mine is Muscat de Beaume de Venise, a heavenly sweet wine made from the muscat grape.

When the dessert is completed, then cheese and fruit are served with port wine. Finally, at the of end the dinner, a whiskey or Cognac is served, and the optional cigar would cap the evening off perfectly.

There is an order to this, as you can see. We have followed the rules of white to red, young to old, light to full bodied, and dry to sweet. As for the highly spirited drinks of 40 percent ABV, they are at the end of the meal.

How you pair the wine is entirely up to you, but bear in mind that you would want it to match the food. You are seeking balance between the food and the wine.

May all your meals be memorable, filled with stimulating conversation, and accompanied by friendships renewed and gained.

DINING ETIQUETTE

IN THIS SECTION, we focus on dining, which is an integral part of social and business interactions. Whether it is formal or informal, if you are a dining neophyte or seasoned veteran, this will be a great learning adventure. From the time you are seated to the end of the dinner and the events in between, you will learn the necessary protocols for seating arrangements, ordering from the menu, tipping procedures, and using correct table manners, like when to start and end a meal. You will feel comfortable with where to place your napkin and how to excuse yourself from the table.

You will wine and dine with distinctly diverse cultures from across the world. Their tastes and manners may or may not be shared by you. Remember the situation and environment you are in and respect, be gracious, and be polite when there are differences. Your newly acquired knowledge will raise your personal dining level and standards and reach the expectations of other dining cultures.

Dining History: When People Ate

The ancient Romans only consumed one meal a day, as this was the best time to ensure digestion would be thorough. In medieval Europe, they enjoyed two meals a day. They had dinner at mid-day and a lighter supper in the evening. Food was sparse and relied on the agrarian economy. Only the ancient Greeks thought of breakfast, which often would be stale bread soaked in wine.

In ancient China, before the Qin and Han dynasties, the populous only ate twice a day because of food shortages and instability of crops and the availability of food. The first meal was at 9 in the morning and the last meal of the day at 4 in the afternoon. By the time of the Han dynasty, the upper class and rulers ate three to four meals a day. With economic development and growth, this was soon the practice of the entire country. Being an agricultural economy, breakfast was at the breaking of dawn, dinner at the end of the day, and lunch was in between.

The Industrial Revolution of the nineteenth century changed the eating hours to suit the work times of the population. It was the 1950s that heralded the popularity of three meals in the United States, and breakfast was the main meal of the day. This was popularized in Europe within a short time. Lifestyles, food stability, and times dictated when people would eat. Some countries would set their times to Central European Time (CET), while others were on Greenwich Mean Time (GMT).

Different time zones are one of the main factors why people eat their meals at different times. Spain uses CET, while many others use GMT. Historical legacy, economic development, and timing affect the times we eat today and how we eat.

Dining Differences: Eating Rituals and Styles

If you live in a modern city, you will see people eating their food in diverse ways, from bowls and plates to banana leaves or communal metallic trays. Throw in the fish knife, meat knife, different forks, and soup spoons, and you can see the utensils mainly used in North America, Australia, New Zealand, and Europe. Forks and spoons are preferred by the Thais and Filipinos, while the Chinese, Japanese, and Korean each have their own set of unique chopsticks. Don't forget the most versatile equipment we humans have: our hands, which are used predominantly for eating in the Middle East, many parts of Africa, and India.

You have a good idea of how complicated eating can be when you add cultural differences and etiquette to this recipe of eating differences. Food is revered because it gives us sustenance to live, and each culture respects that, which is why it is important to understand the rules of etiquette when eating with others.

Appreciating Food That is Simultaneously Offensive and Delightful

Our eating habits are different, and this translates into the foods we eat. The French and Italians eat horses, while the Chinese eat the entire fish, head to tail, and consider chicken feet a delicacy. The Scottish eat haggis, which is made up of the lungs, liver, and heart of a sheep mixed with spices and stock cooked in lamb's stomach, as well as black pudding, which is dried blood fried crispy.

What is one man's poison can be another man's delight. When eating out in different countries, be brave, be bold, and, at times, have a good dose of stomach tablets to calm the nerves. Be adventurous though. When dining, be respectful of how others eat, especially when it is vastly different to our own style. Do not baulk at differences when confronted with them, but exercise respect and grace. It is called etiquette.

How to Set the Table for an Informal Dinner

These are the best, and often unplanned, dinners. It could be a very cozy and warm dinner around the family table with a close friend's family or sitting outside huddled around the BBQ. Whatever the surroundings or the time of year, the most cherished aspect of such dinners are the guests and the time spent together. With that vital focus for an informal dinner table setting, ensure the following three main points.

First, make sure everything that one might possibly need is placed either on the dinner table or close by. If everything is at arm's length, you won't have to get up to fetch forgotten things. This maximizes the time together with the least disruption.

Secondly, use a standard informal dinner setting for your table. The wine glass and drinking water glass go on the right side of the plate, which is the center point. The napkin is placed on the main plate itself. Forks are on the left of the plate, and knives are on the right side of the plate accompanying the soup spoon. The bread plate and butter knife are placed on the left side of the main plate above the forks. The butter knife is placed on top of the bread plate. Although this is the standard for informal dinner settings, they can vary according to your preference. The main feature with informal dinner settings is all cutlery is placed on the table at the same time.

The third point is that if the setting is informal, then match your dinner course and menu in the same manner. The courses should be for a three-course meal, most likely a salad, appetizer, or soup, followed by the main course and then a dessert.

Simple enough, but you would be surprised by how many times people need to get up and down and up and down because of poor planning. Etiquette requires good planning and looking after your guests well.

Menu Considerations for Informal Meals at Home

I remember my mother would always say, "When you invite people to your home and they agree, it is a great privilege for you that they accept your invitation." Hosting a meal with friends in your home is indeed an honor, which requires detailed thoughts and deliberation when planning such an event.

One of my best friends was Scottish. I was invited to his home frequently for a meal with his family. His mother would always write down what she served me whenever I visited for a meal. I asked her one day why she was so detailed, and she replied it was to ensure that I would not eat the same dish twice, as that would be poor etiquette. To this day, I follow this rather fine principle.

If the dinner is for a specific occasion and has a traditional theme, let the guests know. Naturally, all the principles of invitation, like confirming the time, dress code, and plus-one allowance, should be shared in advance.

The food is the star of the evening. The main consideration you should make when planning your meal is to inquire if your guests have any food restrictions. Next, when cooking your meal, think about the cultural and visual aspect of your dish. For example, many cultures when serving fish do not include the tail and the head, only fish that has been filleted. Many might be flabbergasted at the view of a fish head served at the dinner table. When you are going to host a meal at home, be careful not to offer visually off-putting dishes.

Everyone has a different threshold when it comes to spicy food. Thai chili is vastly different to Northern Indian chili or Mexican chili. If you are contemplating making a chili dish, or for that matter, any food that may have a particularly strong flavor intensity, ask your guests if they like that type of food.

There are certain foods that certain cultures will not eat. For example, Hindus will not eat beef, and Muslims and Jewish people will not eat pork. There are many other added limitations when hosting a Jewish friend. They also shy away from any crustaceans, birds with webbed feet like duck, and certain cooking methods. Be aware of them to avoid embarrassment for your guest and yourself.

Pairing your meal with wine is an art. The meal itself could be quite simple, and the pairing of the wine is equally simple if you follow these guidelines. Food that has more of an acidic and salty flavor pairs well with wine because the food makes it more fruity and smoother, less dry and bitter. With food that has more of a sweet, chili, or umami flavor, wine becomes less fruity, drier, and less smooth.

Perhaps this is obvious, but do not forget to make your home clean and tidy, especially the washroom. Always cook a little more then you expect. By doing so, you will not feel the pressure when guests take a second helping, and you do not need to worry if there is enough food.

Perfect, you should be quite ready to entertain guests for an informal meal at home.

Entertaining Options and Etiquette

Time is always fleeting, and our hurried lives sadly reflect us. Think of the last time you said, "This year has zoomed by." Too often, yet we should make ourselves available for one another. Easier said than done. Entertaining is one way of making time with others, and we feel alive enjoying time with our friends and family. This can come in many forms.

One option for entertaining is an impromptu get-together. Order food in from a restaurant and use delivery services to deliver the food to the home. If this is a jointly agreed get-together, then the correct etiquette is to share the cost of the meal ordered. Note that agreeing to host the impromptu gathering does not mean that you have to pay for the entire meal. Guests should be gracious to offer to pay their share.

Another favorite entertaining option in recent times is a potluck. The host prepares the main dish, and the guests bring in supplemental dishes to support the main dish. If you are going to hold a potluck, you should suggest what your guests could bring, as you know who the guests are and if there are any food allergies or restrictions. Be kind enough to make the host's coordination easier.

In both of these scenarios, you may feel that your wine selection could be somewhat limited. Do not feel awkward if you want to let your guests bring their own wine. Simply inform them it is a "bring you own bottle" (BYOB). This way everyone can feel somewhat less restricted, and they can bring whatever they would like to enjoy.

And of course, we then have the classic dinner party, upon which I will spend a bit more time in the sections following. No matter the type of event, always remember there is appropriate etiquette to follow.

How to Set the Table for a Formal Dinner

These types of meals are enormously rewarding when done well and horrendously shocking when done badly. Ensure that you calculate enough time for you to plan, prepare, and execute the evening exceedingly well. Three main points to consider:

First, decide what the menu will be. With a formal dinner, the standard meal can range from six to eight courses. This may take the form of an appetizer, then soup, salad, a starch, a protein, and then finally the dessert.

Point two relates to how we set the table. With a formal table setting, we use either a charger or a service plate. This is placed about one inch from the table's edge, directly in front of where the chair will be. On the left side of the charger, the forks are placed, and there will be several. They may include the appetizer, salad, and main course forks. On the same left side, but slightly above the forks, is the bread plate and butter knife, with the butter knife placed on the bread plate. On the right side of the charger, we have closest to the plate the main course knife, then the salad or starch knife, or both depending on what is being served, then right on the periphery is the soup spoon. Right above the charger, the dessert spoon and fork are placed horizontal to the table and the plate. Above them, you have the individual salt and pepper shakers for each guest on either side of the place card setting. Slightly above the cutlery placed on the right of the charger, we have a combination of drinking glasses for red wine, white wine, and sparkling wine.

The third and last point is to ensure you have the correct wine and food pairing and the wine is chilled and served at the correct temperature. With formal settings, there can be a number of toasts, so it is wise to have enough wine at hand. A final tip with formal dinners is that the cutlery may be removed with each course, whereas in an informal setting, the cutlery remains thoughout the dinner.

Why is it important to set your table out correctly? When everyone follows the same etiquette for formal dining settings, you know what to expect and how to use the cutlery and plates based on their placements. This allows you to correctly follow etiquette as a guest. It is important that you follow protocol as a host too, otherwise it may cause confusion.

Chopstick Technique and Etiquette
The secret to being proficient at using chopsticks is to practice, then practice more, and finally practice even more. You probably will not starve when you need to use them to eat, so remember this when practicing. Since a large majority of Asians uses chopsticks, including the Chinese, Koreans, Japanese, and Vietnamese, you will want to be ready to dine with them confidently.

Here are a few tips on chopstick etiquette to help you feel confident and competent. Please note, however, that due to cultural differences, the following are general guidelines only, and the etiquette may vary by country.

First, learn to hold the chopsticks correctly. There are many videos on social media that you can source as to how to hold chopsticks and how to use them to eat rice especially. Once you've mastered holding the chopsticks correctly, practice at home by picking up pieces of cashews or peanuts. Don't despair if you happen to drop a few pieces; it will become easier with practice.

Chopsticks are symbolic in Asia and etiquette related to them is meaningful and ancient. Here are some important etiquette tips. Avoid waving your chopsticks in the air while eating, and never point the chopsticks at other people. Do not use your chopsticks, the pointed ends where you ate food from, to take food from a communal dish. It used to be the norm to share from the communal dish, but with the new generation and the pandemic, this practice has reduced and changed considerably. Rather than eating directly from the shared dish, use the blunt ends of your chopsticks for serving yourself if there are no serving chopsticks. You simply flip your chopsticks around to use the end that has not been in your mouth to take food from the communal plate.

Nowadays "serving chopsticks" are increasingly popular and used to take food from the serving dishes. They are often a different type or color than the individual chopsticks everyone has at the table. After serving yourself with the "serving chopsticks," return them to the bowl so that others may use them as well. Do not use the serving chopsticks to poke or dig around in communal dishes for the choicest pieces of meat or vegetables.

One should never stand your chopsticks upright in your bowl of rice, as this is symbolic and correlated with funeral rites practiced at the graveyard. Chopsticks placed vertically in a rice bowl look eerily similar to incense sticks placed upright in funeral jars. Chopsticks are always used together, so avoid spearing your food with one chopstick and eating off the end like a huge skewer. Avoid licking or sucking your chopsticks, as this is frowned upon.

When chopsticks are not being used, place them either on a chopstick rest or on your rice bowl with the chopsticks placed side by side. Do not place them in a V-shape.

Do note that the length, size, and shape of Chinese, Japanese, and Korean chopsticks differ greatly. Understandably, chopsticks may not be your cutlery of choice or even third choice, but grin and bear it. Welcome to the global world.

How to Eat Politely with Your Hands

The three main methods of eating food include knives and forks, chopsticks, and our hands. When I mention hands, most of you may be unfamiliar with the etiquette involved in using what we were given by nature.

The three main areas of the world that use their hands to eat more commonly, and where you might be required to use your hands, are in the Middle East, Africa, and India. Each area shares common rules of courtesy, with some differences. Please understand what I term the golden rules. While obvious to those who eat with their hands, they are not to those who seldom or have never eaten with their hands.

Before eating with your hands, ensure they are clean. Cleanliness is paramount, so remember to wash your hands thoroughly. In Africa, you may see two bowls placed in front of you. One is to wash your hands before the meal and the other to wash your hands after the meal.

Never use your left hand at all and use only your right hand. The left hand is used to clean other body parts, and hence considered to be unclean for putting food into your mouth. This is very important to note, and for left-handed people, remember my rules of being conscious of your situation and environment.

Now that the hands are clean, let's get to the most important part of the actual eating. In India, you will most likely be served either roti, naan, or chapati, which is an unleavened bread, with your meal. In the Middle East, they will serve pita bread. In these instances, you can tear off a small piece of either bread you are served and make a small funnel shape. Use that to scoop your food and sauces. In Africa, a corn-styled porridge with a thick consistency is offered. It might be called sadza, pap, fufu, or ghaat, depending on where you are in Africa. With this style of offering, you can make a small ball with your hands and use this to dip into the food and sauces to eat.

Only use your fingertips, and bring the food to your mouth, not your mouth to the food. Do not take large portions, but smaller portions, and do not let the food touch your palms. If possible, do not place your fingers in your mouth. Use your thumb as the lever to push food into your mouth. In all the main regions, you may be either sharing a communal plate or have a personal plate for yourself. If it is a communal plate, only take food right in front of you and never go towards food that is on the opposite side of the communal plate from you.

When I first used my hands to eat, it was a messy affair. I can understand what you may be experiencing. You may think it strange to eat with your hands, especially if you are from Europe or North America. You do eat hamburgers, hotdogs, and chicken wings with your hands, so why not other foods?

Utensil Choice and Order at a Formal Dinner

I can imagine seeing the beads of sweat gathering on your forehead when you are about to sit at your first formal dinner. If your neck has an uneasy tightening, stop right now! Let us do this together, at what appears to be a dreadful predicament for you. The first thing you should do is relax and enjoy the experience. Not many people have the opportunity to enjoy being invited to or hosting a formal dinner, so savor the experience.

In a formal dinner setting, the cutlery, glasses, and charger are all placed on the table at the beginning of the meal. A formal dinner normally has six courses, and in more generous settings, an eight-course dinner is not unheard of.

Seated at the dinner table, right in front of you is the charger plate. To the left of the charger plate are the fork settings normally for the appetizer, salad, and main course. If there are more forks, they could include a fish fork. Always begin from the outside cutlery and work inward. With the knives, the same rule applies. You could have an appetizer, salad, fish, and main course knife with a soup spoon on the outward edge. You will have a fork placed above your plate; this is for your dessert and is used only for dessert. The other knife that you will see is the butter knife. This is the only knife on the left side of your charger. The butter knife is placed on the bread plate and used for taking butter from the butter bowl and placing it on your bread plate.

Here are some helpful and saving grace tips that will be useful. If you are unsure about what to do, then wait a while and observe what the hosts of the evening are doing, see which utensils they are using, and follow their lead. If it is rather difficult to see them, then observe the guest to your left and right and opposite of you. Don't forget your wine manners at the dinner table (page 64)!

Preparations for a Classic Formal Dinner at Home

Size does matter, and you do absolutely need to think about the number of people that your home can accommodate comfortably. Once you've established that, the next consideration that you might want to look at is how formal do you really want to be?

If you are going to be extremely formal, then invitations need to be mailed or sent out in advance. You may also want to consider having serving staff for that evening, and at least three courses should be served. Another expectation is that you will inform the guests of the dress attire and if shoes need to be removed. The whole essence of a formal classic dinner at home is that it is very structured. Do not forget the flowers on the table.

The classic dinner party time begins between 6 and 7 in the evening with cocktails. Dinner is served between 7 and 8 in the evening. Your menu would begin with hors d'oeuvres during the cocktail hour. Dinner could begin with either a starter or soup. Sparkling wine is a good pairing for either and makes a grand statement as the opening salvo of a great dinner.

The next course is normally a salad or fish dish accompanied by a white wine. The main course is normally meat accompanied by a red wine, and this is followed by dessert with a late harvest or sweet wine. Next would be a cheese and fruit tray perhaps with a port or Madeira pairing or with coffee or tea. After dinner drinks could include a whiskey or Cognac, ending a delightful evening with friends. The wines are as important as the food, and correct pairing of food and wine is an art, so do learn about the finer points of wine etiquette (page 64). After all, you deserve the best—you work hard enough.

Seating Order and Position of Guests at a Formal Business Dinner

Many of us will have heard of the expression, "You don't want to sit at the back of the bus." There are many versions as to its origins, but all have a similar meaning at the end: Where you are seated does matter.

In the Western sphere of influence, it is customary to have a rectangular type of table. The host normally sits at the head of the table and seats the guest of honor to their right side and the next guest of significance to their left side. If the guest of honor is a married male, then his spouse will sit to the left side of the host.

As for the other guests, the seating could well be male and female seating alternately. Another approach to seating is to place guests in a way that promotes conversation among them. Couples could be separated as well to encourage more conversation and discussion.

Other cultures differ, and in the Chinese business seating arrangement, the one obvious difference is the shape of the dining table. Chinese formal dining tables are circular in shape. In most instances, a private room is booked for a Chinese business dinner. The host faces the door that serves as the entrance to the private room. The guest of honor still sits to the right of the host and the second guest of honor to the left. If there is a secondary host, their back is facing the door. The seats on the left-hand side of the main table are in order of importance, second, fourth, sixth, and so on, and those on the right are third, fifth, and seventh. Guests are seated, according to their status and relationship with the host of the banquet.

Every country has different seating rules, so always ask before sitting down. It's proper etiquette!

Important Business Client Dinner Etiquette

Why is business dinner etiquette important? The camouflage of a dinner does not belie the real intent of the gathering, and that is to develop and conduct business. The arena may have changed from the boardroom to a restaurant, but the objective is the same.

Business dinner etiquette is formal and important, as it reflects you and shows you to your business colleagues. The way you eat, drink, and conduct yourself is important. It offers insight into you, illuminating your social skills and your understanding of etiquette.

Part of the vital preparation before dinner is to dress appropriately, not overly or underdressed. Never dress in a manner that will embarrass you. Should you be attending as a couple, it would be advised that your partner also be aware of the importance of the event. Arrive on time, and certainly not later than fifteen minutes after the scheduled start time. Always have it clearly emblazoned in your mind the purpose of the dinner, and when engaging in conversation, shy away from controversial topics (page 54).

Now the eating part. The most enjoyable but also the most scrutinized part of the evening. It begins with the seating arrangements; ensure you are seated correctly and, when appropriate, assist those that wish to have their chairs pulled out for them. Leave your elbows off the table (page 112), and always make sure you are very familiar with wine and spirit etiquette (page 64).

If you are not the host, then observe and follow the host's lead and behave accordingly. Remember to use the utensils from outside going inward, and dab the side of your mouth with the napkin before drinking a glass of wine or spirits. Be polite to everyone, including the servers, as this is often the litmus test many use to see how you treat others. Make no mistake—the first business dinner is the one where both sides will scrutinize the most.

When ordering your dinner, you may not be sure if it's acceptable to order a starter or not. Observe and watch what the host orders, and then you can follow suit. When ordering, order something simple to eat that does not require a complicated set of skills to enjoy. Wait until everyone's food has arrived, then only begin eating after the host invites everyone to do so.

When eating, do not chew with your mouth open and certainly do not hold a conversation with food in your mouth. A few more points are to engage in general conversation with the other guests and keep your cell phone silent and out of sight. This means you should not be texting, sending emails, or checking the news on your phone.

Apart from this lengthy list of dos and don'ts, enjoy your dinner. If it you are in another country for your business dinner, then your learning curve will be very high, but you can do it. The principles of politeness and social graces will be similar, even if the cutlery is different.

Procedure and Timing for Sitting at the Table

Timing can make a difference toward success or failure. How many times have you thought to yourself, "If I had only left a few minutes earlier, what a big difference it would have made." We should all be aware of the importance of timing, especially at dinner. One should always wait for the host to announce that dinner is being served, and then proceed to be seated.

If the dinner is informal or formal, it is always polite to ask the host where they would prefer the guests be seated. In an informal setting, it is somewhat more relaxed, and seating changes can be made quite simply and easily.

In a formal setting, the host could be at the table and, as the guests arrive at the dining room table, indicate where guests should sit. There may also be name cards placed on the table so guests will know where to sit without having to ask the host.

For gentlemen in a formal setting, always remember before you do sit down to ensure that you ask the ladies, should there be any ladies seated on either side of you, if they would like you to assist. If so, please pull the chair out for them and seat them accordingly, then seat yourself. If they prefer to seat themselves, then you should go ahead and sit yourself down. For the ladies, be prepared to politely request or decline assistance in sitting when it is offered.

One should always enter the seat from the right-hand side and sit. When standing up and leaving the table, one should leave from the left side of the chair. When you leave from your chair from the left side, you cannot accidently bump the guest's fork.

If you are wearing a jacket, please don't forget to unbutton your jacket before sitting. Your jacket should be loose and unbuttoned when seated. Likewise, if you are wearing a skirt or dress, it is highly recommended that you do not forget to use the palms of your hands to smooth any creases out from the back of your dress or skirt, before being seated (page 50). Oh, by the way, don't begin to eat until the host has announced to the group to begin or has completed all formalities prior to dinner.

Procedure and Timing for Starting Your Meal

As a young boy, I recall we had to wait until everyone was seated at the table, and then one of our parents would tell us that we could begin dinner. Manners are so vital and should be taught at home, just like this important one.

At any formal seated dinner, one must wait for the host to announce to the guests, "Please, let's begin dinner." It is highly improper to start dinner as soon as you sit down and not wait for everyone. The reason is that there may be certain traditions, like a short speech, holding of hands to say grace, or a few words of thanks, that take place before the meal. So do not be in such a hurry, or you might be called a glutton for wanting to eat immediately. It is hard to wait, especially after looking at such delicious dishes right before your ravenous eyes, but you must.

At an informal dinner, you should still always wait for all of the guests to sit down and for the host to announce that dinner can begin. There may be a specific order where older people and children are served first then other guests.

In the case of a buffet, it is an accepted practice that when you go up and select your meal, there is no need to wait for others. You can begin immediately as soon as you sit down. The logic is that your food will get cold before the others return.

When you are dining in a restaurant, wait until all the guests are served at your table before beginning to eat. At a private dinner party, when your host or hostess picks up their utensils to eat, then you may eat. Do not start before this unless the host insists that you start eating.

Patience is a virtue and a quality that many people consider desirable.

When are Ladies and Gentlemen Expected to Stand?

At my all-boys school, when sitting anywhere on our school grounds chatting with fellow classmates or relaxing in the sun, you were expected to stand up and greet any passing visitor, as they were guests at your school. Whether they were parents of a fellow schoolmate or a potential student, we were expected to be welcoming and show respect and politeness. Either way, most of the guests would be older than you, and standing up was a sign of welcome. However, as I keep referencing, times change. This may seem outdated for some readers, but not all. You must evaluate the situation and environment you are in before deciding to stand.

You may be at an informal event at someone's home or a venue when the hosts come by with a fellow guest they wish to introduce to you. It would be polite to stand up for such introductions. By standing up, you immediately let the person being introduced to you know you are showing respect to them and the host. When meeting someone for the very first time, be it at a dinner, boardroom, or reception, I stand up and introduce myself.

As a gentleman, whenever a lady joins or leaves a group, you can stand up on each occasion or you can stand for her introduction and final departure. Either of these practices are acceptable. If the husband of the wife is present and does not stand whenever she leaves, then it is good form to follow his lead and not stand up every time. What about ladies? Actually, all the same practices apply, except there is no need to stand up for other ladies. You do not need to stand every single time others arrive and leave a group. Only once upon introduction and at the end of the meeting or saying goodbye. Ladies, if you feel it unnecessary that gentlemen stand up every time, then you should politely inform them by saying, "Gentlemen, thank you, but no need to stand up for me every time."

In a business environment, one should stand up when meeting clients, when being introduced, and at the end of the meeting. When a senior member, like the CEO or director of the company, enters your office, it is professional etiquette to stand up and greet them.

Standing up and rising to the occasion is an extension of politeness and respect towards others. Ladies and gentlemen, when appropriate, let's all rise to the occasion.

Cell Phone Etiquette

Many argue that the world is on steroids when it comes to the breakneck speed and pace of modern-day living. We have this "baby," also called a cell phone, mobile, or smartphone, attached awfully close, within arm's reach of us, almost 24/7. We check mail, texts, news, recipes, and a multitude of other interests on the phone at all times. That includes dinner, right?

The answer is no. Dinner begins with the phone being placed out of sight, not on the table or close by where it can be seen. Rather, place it in your bag or the inside of your jacket, on silent mode (not vibrate). I have witnessed hugely embarrassing moments when, in the middle of a speech, a phone rings or vibrates loudly. The owner of the phone really wishes they could disappear into the deepest crevice possible.

Are there exceptions to this seemingly draconian approach? There always are. Preemptive preparation is what I term it. If you are expecting a call, let your intended caller know that you will not be available to answer calls at certain times. When possible, record a message on your phone to that effect.

If you cannot do this because you are expecting an extremely important call, need to respond to urgent texts you are expecting, or are waiting for a time-sensitive email for that matter, it would be good manners to inform the host that, in such an event, you may have to unexpectedly leave the table. Once aware of your intrusions, the host will take no slight and may even make arrangements for your situation. The host can accommodate you by seating you in a less conspicuous seating place. Then you can disappear briefly without disturbing the evening's proceedings. It is also not a bad idea to inform your fellow guests who are sitting to your left and right, asking them to excuse you when you will need to leave the table unexpectedly.

If you have to respond to calls, texts, and emails, then do so in one session. That way you are not subjecting other guests to a continual "musical chairs" cabaret where you are up and down and up and down like a jack-in-the-box. You do not wish to be labeled as the inconsiderate one. Keep the calls to a minimum, and let the caller know you will return their call after the meal. If you know you will be receiving several important calls, then you need to decide if you can attend the event or not, especially for formal events. Continual disturbances of this nature are very poor etiquette toward your hosts and fellow guests, so try to refrain from being guilty of this type of behavior.

Awareness of situation and environment is vital here. Many people and groups in countries located in Asia do not mind if there are phones being used at informal or semi-formal dinners, but they do mind at formal events. It is the norm certainly in China, Hong Kong, Korea, and Vietnam. Business cards are being relegated for a myriad of software connection options like WhatsApp, or they are set up as electronic business cards. You will need a phone to scan the card and save the contact details. Smartphones are now being used to take photographs of the food and friends, and sharing photos with one another is paramount. It is not an easy request to set aside your cell phone.

In all instances, if you do need to take a call, the very least you can do is to excuse yourself and take the call privately to avoid disturbing others.

Buffet Etiquette

There are several horror videos that have circulated around social media platforms showing buffet diners battling their way through hordes to get their meal. It is chaotic, and one might be forgiven for thinking these people have not had a meal in days. There are scenes that show diners using their entire plate to scoop up the shrimp from a bain-marie instead of using a set of tongs. Certainly not a practice we want to condone.

Buffet etiquette rules are simple. Buffets are quite common at weddings, golf tournament dinners, fundraising dinners, and other events. There is an order as to which table can approach the buffet to get their meal. The instructions are normally delivered by the Master of Ceremonies for the event, and they will announce whose turn it is to go. We should adhere to this order.

When you are at the buffet table, do use the serving utensils that they have provided, and the portion that you serve yourself for the first time should always be a modest, not necessarily large, serving. You can always go back for a second helping, and this way you do not waste food while figuring out which dish is your preference.

When you are serving yourself from the buffet tray, always serve from the area that is nearest to you. This will avoid spills. Oftentimes, there are two opposite facing lines serving themselves from the same tray, but people should help themselves from the side they are standing on.

I would recommend that if you are going to go for a second serving, begin with a fresh plate.

Napkin Placement and Use

Distinct cultures eat in unusual ways, and not everyone uses a napkin. Napkin use depends on the eating style. Eating with hands is different to chopsticks and the standard knife and fork. If one uses hands, then a napkin will be used differently than it is when eating with utensils. It would be difficult to use a napkin after every bite when hands are used to eat. Normally, one would use a napkin at the end of the meal to clean hands, and then hands are more thoroughly washed in the washroom. There are times when a hand basin and water are brought to the table for hand washing.

Generally, as soon as you sit down at the table, you should place the napkin on your lap, covering both thighs. This is preferable, but the napkin can also be placed on one side, usually the right. When you place the napkin on your lap, it is an indication that the meal is about to begin. Napkins should always be used, when necessary and possible.

Please observe the manner of holding the napkin. A linen napkin is used frequently during the meal by guests, but not as if it's a washing towel for wiping your face. It is used to blot or pat but not to wipe your face. When you are blotting or patting, you will use your index finger and thumb to hold a small section of the napkin in a horizontal position to the table and wipe the specific area. These areas are normally at the corner of your mouth. Blot or pat the side of your mouth before drinking your wine, otherwise you will leave a greasy oil stain on the rim of the glass.

If you need to leave the table during the meal, place the napkin down loosely to the left-hand side of your plate but ensure that there are no visible stains for other guests to see. Don't leave the napkin on the back of your chair and never on the seat of the chair. It is unsightly and certainly not hygienic.

How to Eat Bread and Butter at a Restaurant

At a restaurant in North America or Europe, you are often served bread prior to the meal. The server usually delivers some freshly baked or heated bread to your table shortly after you are seated. If you are the host, you should pick up the breadbasket and offer it to the other guests first before serving yourself. Pick up a single piece of bread or bun and place it on your bread plate. Thereafter, take your butter knife, which is normally placed either to the side of your bread plate or on top of the bread plate. Using your butter knife, take a small piece of butter and place that piece of butter on one side of your bread plate. Then break the piece of bread that is on your plate into bite-size pieces. One at a time, butter the pieces of bread using the butter you already placed on the side of your bread plate. Do not take butter directly from the butter plate to butter your bread. Do not butter the entire piece of bread without breaking the bread into bite-size pieces. You are not making sandwiches. This is a major faux pas.

What to Do if You Drop Cutlery at a Restaurant

Accidents do happen, and if you drop any cutlery or your napkin, the instinctive behavior is to bend down and pick it up. At a formal dinner, etiquette dictates that you not do this. Rather, you should call the attention of a server and let them know that you have dropped a particular piece of cutlery or napkin and would they be kind enough to replace it for you.

Kindly indicate to them where the cutlery or napkin is on the floor. The professional server will be more than happy to retrieve the cutlery and take it away. The logic behind this is that you do not want to place cutlery that has dropped on the floor onto the table where you and other guests eat. Likewise with napkins, since you use them to dab or wipe your mouth, it makes no sense to use one that has fallen onto the floor.

Dining Etiquette for Drinking

In certain cultures, like Korea, you should never pour and refill your own wine or spirit glass. If you must do this, it means that those having a meal with you are not following correct etiquette. Because you must never pour your own drink, always be alert throughout the meal as to whether your neighbor's cup or wine glass needs refilling. If it is less than half full, add to it. If yours is less than half full, your neighbor is obliged to refill it. If he or she does not, do not refill it yourself. Instead, pour a little more drink into your neighbor's glass, even if it doesn't really need it. They will understand and then pour you a drink.

Ensure you know how to hold the wine and spirit glasses correctly. When you are holding a wine glass with a stem, never hold the glass by the bowl. Always hold it by the stem of the glass or the base. If you hold the wine glass by the bowl and your hands are covered in grease, you will smear the bowl of the wine glass. The greasy and oily stains are not a very pretty sight. To prevent stains from appearing on the rim of your glass, always dab the corners of your mouth with your napkin before you take your next sip.

Whiskey glasses are less taxing, as one cannot see a huge bulb. It makes drinking whiskey less stressful. Still, bear in mind that if you have eaten food, whether it is nuts or little snacks, it is always a good idea to dab your mouth with the napkin before you take another drink.

In England, the famous pubs are known for witty banter and laughter. One unwritten but strongly practiced etiquette is if someone buys you a drink, or affectionately known as "a round" or "my shout," you should reciprocate before leaving by, at the very least, offering to buy "a round." Your colleagues may not accept your generosity and say that next time you can buy the first round, but at least you offered. Never leave without making it clear that you did offer to buy your round.

One should never pressure those individuals who clearly state they have had enough for the evening. It may be tempting for the sake of continued mirth and laughter, but responsible drinking is vital and non-negotiable. This principle should also include stopping those who are clearly inebriated from drinking any further. Above all, ensure that those people who are drinking can return to their home safely. Better to be safe than sorry.

Engaging Your Guests at the Dinner Table

The most important word here is "guests," and you must select them with care and deliberation. You invited them, so the common denominator among all of them is you. You know each of them intimately, their likes, dislikes, interests, and topics that should avoided. Armed with that very important knowledge, you are, in the true sense of the word, the "general" that can maneuver the conversation in a skillful way that will include all guests and allow each one to sparkle with vibrant and engaging conversation.

I normally break the evening conversation into three parts. The first part is the "icebreaker," per North American parlance. This is the initial meeting where most of the guests are sussing out the other guests and environment. The mood is reserved, as no one particularly wants to make a wrong step. Before dinner, the guests would most likely mingle in the lounge, patio, or even the kitchen. They are not all seated together, and this allows you as the host to take the initiative and introduce guests who you think have a common thread. You can glide in with topics on recent holidays, interests you know they both have, or experiences that are common. After the first part is over, dinner is served at the table and the formalities are over and people are more relaxed.

Part two begins with the start of the meal, and food is an excellent topic. It is universal, as we all eat food in different measures and enjoy it. Ask open-ended questions, like where was the best and worst meal you have ever had? Why? Rather than asking one person, perhaps select all the ladies and let them take turns among themselves, then move on to the men. You could select guests to your left and then right. Conversation is usually flowing rather well now.

Part three is easier as a result of the flowing conversation. Finding a topic of current interests that affects everyone provides a smooth transition. Normally after this, small conversations tend to break out on the table among the guests. If not, try sharing a personal experience and ask for the opinion of the other guests. It might be about going to the store the other day and buying the bottle of wine that everyone is enjoying now and explaining why that particular wine was chosen. Then use the wine to transition to talk about their wine experiences. From there it's easy to glide into talk of holidays and travel.

Sound rehearsed? It is. Better having a plan for conversation than experiencing extended periods of uneasy silence. Normally in my experience, after the second stage, the guests are well oiled and steaming ahead rather smoothly.

Of course, avoid topics of politics, money, and religion (page 55), as they can ignite as quickly as dry grass on a sweltering summer day.

How to Handle Group Orders at a Restaurant

Far too often, many of us fall prey to succumbing to the will of the masses when ordering in a group. We do not want to appear awkward and miserly, so as the saying goes, "Go with the flow."

Imagine at an informal get-together, the group decides to order several appetizers together and share them before going to another venue or activity. In such instances, there is a "leader of the pack" as it were, and they will ask what everyone thinks and might even suggest a few dishes themselves or ask everyone to select a dish. The problem arises with allergies, rather expensive dishes that you don't eat, and an allocated budget for the evening. If you are the leader, it would be good etiquette to set the rules out. Establish the number of dishes to be shared and ask if there are any allergies. Be open and state, as an example, "There are six of us, so we will all share the cost. Let's ensure everyone can eat everything we order." This way no one feels excluded or bitter about having to pay their share and not eating. If you are not the leader, it's perfectly fine to speak up and ask about the group's expectations. Drinks should always be separate, as there are non-drinkers often in a group, and it is grossly unfair for them to share the cost of drinks.

Picture another scenario of your group going out for a dinner. Upon arrival at the restaurant, menus are presented and some order a starter, but you don't feel like ordering one. Should you have to? In the majority of cases for group gatherings like this, the North American parlance is "going Dutch" or "AA制 (zhì)" in China, which means you pay for what you order. This makes it rather easy to order what you like only without feeling obliged to order a full three-course meal. My suggestion is if you order a main meal and no appetizer while others in the group have, request the server bring your main meal with the appetizers. This way you are all eating together.

Dinner with Vegetarian Guests

A guest is a guest and should not be defined by what they eat. The unbroken rule when entertaining guests is to ensure they feel comfortable, respected, and able to enjoy the time spent in your company. Your behavior should be gracious and considerate. It is not a difficult and insurmountable task for you to have one meal void of any meat. It might even do you some good healthwise and provide a new experience at the same time. Every country in the world has vegetarians, and many of my friends are perfectly healthy vegetarians. Their food, when I am fortunate enough to be invited, is a true feast for the palate. The aromas, texture, and flavor of the food are divine and enticing.

Knowing that you will be having dinner with a vegetarian, it would be highly recommended that you identify what type of vegetarian they actually are. There are several categories of vegetarians, and this can impact the food that you can order or cook. The thoroughbred vegetarian, commonly know as vegan, does not eat any animal or dairy products, including eggs. A variation of the thoroughbred vegetarian, called lacto-vegetarians, are individuals who do not eat any meat or eggs, but will eat dairy products. Lacto-vegetarians are not to be confused with lacto-ovo vegetarians who will not eat meat, but they will eat dairy products and eggs. Let's not forget the fish lovers, or pescatarians, who will not eat meat, but do eat fish, eggs, and all dairy products. Ovo-vegetarians maintain a diet that excludes all animal-based foods except for eggs, including whole eggs, egg whites, and egg-containing foods like egg noodles and mayonnaise. Flexitarians, or flexible vegetarians, are a group whose diet includes a high proportion of plant-based foods, but they will still eat small amounts of meat and other animal products occasionally.

You need to decide if you will be cooking a meal at home or inviting your guest to a restaurant. My suggestion is, unless you are quite adept at cooking vegetarian dishes, you should consider the latter option. Before deciding which vegetarian restaurant to eat at, confirm the type of vegetarian diet that your guest follows. Having established that, then call ahead to confirm if the vegetarian restaurant you are considering offers dishes that would suit your guest. The last thing you want is to go to a vegetarian restaurant, but discover that your friend cannot eat there because of their particular food preferences. A brief note: There are vegetarians that do not eat heated or cooked vegetables, only raw vegetables (raw vegan diet). This makes your selection very easy indeed.

The choice of restaurant should not be stressful, and one way to alleviate any rising tide of stress is to ask your guest if they have a preferred vegetarian restaurant. If they can recommend one, then your potential headache is solved, as you can be assured that they have eaten there before.

Certainly, before the date of the meal, discuss the choices with them in advance. They may surprise you by saying it's perfectly fine to go to a restaurant where they serve meat. They will order something vegetarian. If this offer is made, you should decide if you feel that would be appropriate, such as if there are other non-vegetarian guests.

When ordering wine, if your guests do not eat eggs, you should ask the wine steward for wines that have not used casein, the principal protein in milk, for "fining" the wine. Milk is not added to wine; it is the whites of the egg, if used at all. Most of it is filtered out from the wine, but minute traces can remain. Just a thought for you to consider when ordering the wine.

Following these very considerate steps, your etiquette is sure to make your vegetarian guests feel welcome.

How to Eat Lobster Elegantly

Lobster is the bane of many diners. One might love the thought of eating lobster, hate the arduous work necessary to eat it, or prefer not to eat it at all.

Imagine you are at a dinner and the set menu gives you no choice except lobster for the main course. It might be a test to see how you cope, so knowing your options is always an advantage.

Always observe what the host is doing. If they request a bib, then you should too, as eating lobster can be difficult and messy at times. If the host brings a specialized set of eating cutlery for you prior to the lobster being served, then chances are it will be a grappling affair. But have no fear! You will turn the eating process into a smooth, fluid dance.

You might be given the specialized equipment, much like a surgeon's tools, which makes it easier for you to get every piece of lobster meat out and into your mouth. The lobster cracker looks similar to a nutcracker, but you use it to crack the lobster shell where you see fit, generally the claws. Then there is the lobster pick, which you use to pick the lobster meat from the crevices in the claws. Remember to always eat the lobster meat from your main fork, not the lobster pick.

There is a shell bowl where you can place the empty shells once you have gleaned every piece of delicious lobster meat from within. Do not place your shells on the table. You will be provided with a bowl of water that has a slice of lemon inside to clean your hands and even some moist and warm napkins to wipe your hands. I prefer to still go the washroom and wash my hands thoroughly after cleaning them with the bowl and moist napkin, but that is your personal choice.

The order in which you eat the lobster has no rules. You may eat it in whichever order you wish. You could begin by removing the small claws, then proceed to the large claws and the lobster tail for the finale. Chewing the claws is a personal favorite, but if you do decide to chew it, then do it silently and elegantly. You can then proceed to the body by slicing it into two halves. When lobster is served at formal dinners, you will find the lobster is already precracked and cut into halves for you.

When eating the meat from the tail, lift the lobster meat from the shell using your knife and fork, place it on your plate, then cut and eat one piece at a time. The lobster may be served with hot butter on the side for you or as a lobster thermidor with a bechamel sauce thickened with flour. In these types of situations, it is easier to eat the lobster, as most of the work to unshell the lobster has been done for you. You may have the claws, but they have been precracked most of the time.

If you have the choice of lobster to select from, here is a tip. There are two main types of lobster. The hard-shell lobster requires more effort, but the meat is firmer and more flavorful. The other type is the "shedder," or soft-shell, lobster, which has an easier shell to crack, but the meat is less flavorful. Also, the amount of meat is decidedly reduced, since the lobster has not yet reached its full maturity. The choice is yours.

I hope you enjoy your first lobster; it is truly addictive when paired with Champagne.

How to Eat Raw Oysters Elegantly

There are many types of oysters to select from at a restaurant. Whichever variety you do select, the oysters need to be shucked. Let us go through the ritual together.

You look at the menu and you decide which variety you would like. There are several oyster options depending on where you are dining. The more popular ones are the Pacific oysters, also known as the Japanese, creuse (France), and Miyagi. They are on the sweet side with a creamy and herbaceous taste. Then there is the Atlantic oyster, also known as the Eastern oyster or virginica. It is larger than the Pacific oyster and has a more briny, crisp, clean, and mineral flavor. Another oyster to consider is the Kumamoto oyster. They are small with a briny, nutty, sweet and melon taste and finish.

I suggest a very dry white wine to pair with your oysters. Personally, a very dry pinot grigio or Champagne is my choice. Once again, everyone's palate is different, so experiment with different wines and, of course, different oysters to find your favorite combination.

The oysters should arrive at your table already shucked, so you don't need to worry about that step. Many people who enjoy eating oysters raw will have some condiments to accompany the oysters. That could consist of simple lemon juice that you squeeze from the piece of lemon provided. There is also the choice of horseradish, a cocktail sauce, mignonette sauce, or a champagne mignonette sauce to accompany the oysters.

When you are served the oysters, they will be on a bed of ice and inside the shell there is some oyster juice pooled. You can add your preferred condiment inside the oyster shell, then tilt the wider bottom edge of the oyster, ensuring you don't spill any juices or condiment sauce, and slide the contents into your mouth. Alternatively, you can use a tiny fork to scoop the meat out and eat the oyster that way. These are the two main options to eat oysters.

With the oyster in your mouth, begin to chew at the oyster rather than swallowing it whole. By chewing into the oyster, the combination of the oyster meat flavor, the pooled briny juice, and the condiments offers a sensational flavor profile. After removing the meat from the shell, I prefer having a separate plate specifically to discard the shells rather than placing them back onto the bed of ice.

Enjoy the classic combination of oysters and Champagne!

How to Eat Bone-In Chicken Elegantly

Chicken is the most versatile meat. It can be cooked in so many assorted styles: deep fried, roasted, steamed, stewed, grilled, and baked, to name a few. It is eaten all over the world. With it comes the perennial question: Do we, can we, should we use our hands when eating chicken if it has bones? The simple answer is yes, but that comes with some caveats.

At a formal dinner, chicken is eaten with a knife and fork, as it is unlikely you will be given pieces of chicken with bones in them. Most likely your chicken will be served roasted, stewed, baked, grilled, or steamed rather than deep fried. It should be easily eaten without using your hands.

At an informal meal, you should begin to use the knife and fork to remove the majority of the meat, and then for the remaining bones and meat you can use your hands. Using your thumb and index finger for the drumstick is quite an easy operation, but for other parts, it does require some delicate maneuvering. Don't place the bones in your mouth and suck at the bones. Privately on your own, feel free to indulge, but in company, definitely do not do this.

At a BBQ, I believe this should be an all-hands-on-deck occasion. Similarly, at a very informal gathering where deep-fried chicken is served, your hands will be required. A little trick when eating chicken wings is to hold the wings with your two hands in between the thumb and index finger at either ends of the wing. Then holding one side firmly, apply a little pressure to the opposite side and twist the wing in a forward motion. This will break the cartilage on the chicken wing, then you can easily remove one of the wing bones. This simple action makes it so much easier to eat chicken wings.

Always consider where you are and who you are eating with before deciding to use your hands. Watch the host for clues, as they are always a good thermometer in terms of how informal you can be.

If the Food is Not to Your Palate or Taste, How Do You Politely Tell the Host?

The simple answer is you do not.

Tastes and flavors are subjective. What you think is awful could well be perfectly cooked and considered a delicacy. It just might not be tailored to your specific tastes or you are not used to it. It would be the height of rudeness and an expression of ingratitude to tell them that their efforts to feed you is not palatable and that the food is simply not good enough.

This can be an extremely difficult situation, as you don't want your host to feel embarrassed, humiliated, and awkward. Hence, the wisest strategy is to take a little portion of each offering at the beginning if you are helping yourself to food in a buffet or potluck style setting. If you like the dish, you can take more during a second serving. In this manner, you can explore, digest, and see which dish is more to your palate when trying dishes from other cultures.

You may also face a situation where the host will serve you food on your plate, especially what they consider to be the choicest cuts or a special dish for you as the guest of honor. If the dish is not to your taste, just don't finish it. Politely let them know you are so full that you couldn't eat another bite while thanking them for the invite.

In a formal dinner, you may not have a choice, as the food is served on your plate in advance. You perhaps could eat what you like on the plate and have a morsel of what you don't like. Don't mention anything; it will become obvious and there is no need to highlight the fact that it was not to your preference.

I remember a time when I was the guest of honor and they served a soup. It was delicious in flavor and texture. As I slowly ate my soup, I noticed what was clearly the limb of a young baby tortoise. It was tortoise soup, after all. My host pointed out to me that for the guest of honor, they had chosen the best part of the tortoise. There was really no way out except to eat it, which I did. It was not something I would choose to eat again, but it was an experience and no loss of face for my host.

As a host, you should take into consideration the food you do serve and ask in advance if you are not sure if the food will be palatable to all of the guests.

How to Handle Spilled Food During a Meal

Accidents do happen and come in many forms, from minor to major. When accidents occur on the dinner table during a meal, as the host you want to ensure the guest does not feel silly, awkward, embarrassed, and, above all, not physically hurt.

There are two main types of spills: liquid and food. Both are equally pressing in urgency. Liquid spills can leave stain marks on clothes or linens if not dealt with promptly, and hot liquids can cause burns or scalding. With foods, the same principles apply. Food can stain or cause pain if it is warm and hot, like soup.

From the perspective of the host, your guest will most likely feel agitated and embarrassed that it happened, so helping to deal with it discreetly and quickly will smooth out any anxious moments. Be calm throughout. Confirm they are not injured, especially in the case of hot liquids. The guest who caused the spill may offer to pay for the cleaning, and as the host, you should graciously decline. If the guest insists and you feel this would make them more comfortable, as there are other guests present, openly you can accept, but after let them know in private that there is no need. I would suggest having a spray that can clean any red wine spills on the tablecloth or on any clothing; it is very handy indeed.

The important factor is to try and observe the setting and reduce any possible situations where spills can easily occur. This could mean placing wine glasses in a certain place or ensuring there is space in between guests. Perhaps you could gracefully inform guests which direction to follow when passing food, avoid overfilling their dishes or topping the wine glasses, and have towels or gloves easily available when it is time to serve from hot plates. This will reduce the risk of spills and other accidents.

As a guest, if you spill food or liquid onto the table, you must contain the spill promptly. More often than not, this means using your napkin, especially if it is on the table. Remain calm and remember that there is no need to raise your voice.

If you have spilled anything onto another person, before you touch them, apologize and offer to help: "I am so sorry, can I help you?" This is very important, especially if you are a gentleman and you have spilled anything onto a lady. If they reply yes, then certainly reach out to help. If the response is "No, I can manage, accidents do happen," then at the very least provide a clean napkin and offer to have the piece of clothing professionally cleaned.

If you drop a morsel onto the table, use your napkin to clean it up. Then catch the eye of a server if you are at a restaurant, pass the soiled napkin to the server, and request a new one. If at a home, the same would apply, but you might get up and remove the stained napkin in the kitchen, and the hosts will likely assist and get you a new napkin.

If a guest sitting next to you spills food or liquid, it is good manners to help immediately, especially with elderly guests. Accidents happen, and thankfully spills at the dinner table are not hardly life threatening. So, be calm and, as soon as possible, continue with the revelry of the occasion.

Elbow Placement During a Meal

Historically, it was not uncommon to place tabletops on a log or tree stump, and I imagine it still happens in many parts of the world. If you were to put your elbows on this type of table, the likelihood of the table flipping because of the pressure exerted by your elbows would be extremely high. The stability of the table is less than desirable, and hence it was the original reason why elbows were not permitted on the table. The reasoning is pragmatic, as no one wants to pick up their food from the floor and eat it.

Elbows should be always at your side when eating. Your wrists should be on the edge of the table. In this position you are not slouching in an unattractive manner. The salient point is that, when eating, your elbows cannot be on the table under any circumstances. As times change, it appears to be widely accepted that after dinner when engaging in conversation with someone opposite or beside you, you can have your elbows on the table. This offers the appearance of being at ease and more casual in approach. If you do decide to have your elbows on the table after the meal, don't use them as a prop to clasp your hands together and hold your head up.

If you are attending a naval dinner, there are exceptions to where the elbows should be placed and when. At a naval dinner, you might see certain navy personnel with their elbows on the table. One elbow indicates the individual crossed the Cape of Good Hope or the Cape of Storms. Both elbows mean they have sailed past both. Navy and adventures are synonymous with tradition, privileges, and etiquette.

How to Respond When Your Mouth is Full

Having a meal should be enjoyable and free of the stresses of the world. When enjoying a meal with friends, certain rules of etiquette allow it to be stress-free, including how to hold a conversation around the process of eating.

Conversation between friends is expected during a meal. When do you ask or answer the questions? If there are two or more of you, some can be holding the conversation while the others eat and listening intently. If you are asked a question while you are eating, should you answer with food in your mouth? Certainly not. Look the person in the eye graciously, place either one of your palms or your napkin over your mouth to indicate that you are eating, and perhaps nod your head, but do not speak. When you have finished the food in your mouth, you may then answer. The person that asked you the question will understand and either wait for you or move the conversation to another with plans to come back to you later.

Some general eating rules are do not speak with food in your mouth and do not chew with your mouth open. Besides being rude, there are also the safety and biological reasons for why you should not speak if your mouth has food in it. By not speaking, you are preventing yourself from choking. Your epiglottis is like a valve located at root of your tongue, and it either closes to allow food to go into your stomach or opens to allow air into your windpipe. When you are breathing or speaking, it remains open, allowing air into your lungs. When you swallow, it closes to prevent food from getting into your windpipe. If you are eating and talking at the same time, you may choke yourself. Two tips: Only ask questions to a person if they do not have food in their mouth and know about the Heimlich maneuver to clear an airway in the event that choking occurs.

What to Do if Your Guests Eat Slowly

All guests eat at different speeds. I've found that those who come from a large family tend to eat their food faster. Food was often a premium when they were younger, and slow eaters in the family did not fare well with their portions. The opposite could reasonably apply to slower eaters; they often come from small families since there were fewer members to contest the food supply.

There are two stages that I have found useful. Stage one, which I term the preemptive stage, is when you try and remove all obstacles that may further delay your guest from finishing their meal in a timely manner. You take the initiative and direct the conversation, not necessarily to dominate but to be more vocal. Direct the conversation where your guest wants to hear more, and this allows them to eat and listen. Perhaps limit their conversation during the meal and wait until after the meal to engage in longer conversation with them. This is a rather drastic position to take, but in the case of exceptionally slow eaters, it works.

Stage two involves adjusting your eating habits. During the meal, if it becomes apparent that guests are slow eaters, you may want to slow your rate of consumption to match them. If you have finished, but do not want your plate to be removed, leave some food on your plate and place your knife and fork in the eight and four o'clock positions. The server will not remove your plate until they see your guests finish their meals. Then you can then quickly polish off the last bits of your meal on your plate.

They say timing is important, and this is an excellent example.

Cutlery Placement Signals

We can all identify signs: stop signs, go signs, exit signs, and gestures. One sign we rarely think much of is the way we place our knife and fork on our plate. This offers a signal to the servers who kindly look after us, showing them what they should do with our plates and cutlery.

During the meal, while pausing or munching away, you will generally place the fork, which is held in your left hand, and the knife, held in your right hand, back onto the plate with the fork overlapping the knife. If the person you are having the meal with is an extraordinarily slow eater, it would be impolite of you to finish your meal too early, so you may wish to accompany the guest while they eat. To prevent a server from removing your plate too soon, ensure the position of your cutlery is correct.

Leave a little food on your plate, then place the base of your fork at an eight o'clock position and the base of the knife at the four o'clock position to signal to the server that you have not yet finished the meal.

When you have finished a course, place your fork and knife together with the fork and knife aimed at the twelve o'clock position and the handles at the six o' clock position. Should they be placed incorrectly, your server will not remove your plate. Even if you have finished that course, they will not act until the placing of your knife and fork indicates you are done. Forgetting will cause the entire dinner party to wait for you before they serve the next course.

You may be curious about why this is important. Well, there are several reasons, but I will focus on the most important one. Often, there are several courses for dinner. After everyone finishes one course, then the next course is served to everyone at the same time. Here, the signals play an important role. The position in which you place your knife and fork on the plate helps the servers keep the courses moving.

At high-end restaurants, the servers are professionally trained, certainly the case with Michelin star restaurants. Giving the correct sign to servers is good etiquette. For your guests, they will appreciate that you are not rushing them to complete their meal nor delaying their meal with conflicting signs.

Ways to Indicate You Have Finished Your Meal at a Restaurant

We eat in three major ways, using either cutlery, chopsticks, or hands. Each calls for a different way to indicate to your server that you have finished with your meal.

Servers at restaurants generally keep a close eye on their guests to ensure good service. In popular and busy restaurants, they keenly observe your table so they can estimate when your table will be free. In the hospitality world, a table is called a cover, and the more covers a restaurant does in one sitting, the more income they make. Not that they will chase you out, but they will know when you are finished.

In most countries, when you are eating with your knife and fork, the best way to indicate you have finished is to place you knife and fork together in the six o'clock vertical position in the middle of your plate. The sharp pointed side of your knife and the prongs of the fork face twelve o'clock and the handles point at six o'clock. In certain parts of the United States, they also adopt the four o'clock position in addition to the six o'clock position.

When using chopsticks in a Chinese, Korean, Japanese, or similarly styled restaurant, place your chopsticks together on your bowl either at a twelve o'clock or three o'clock position. If you have a Japanese bento box, the same rule applies. There is also the option to place your chopsticks in chopstick holders on your right-hand side, if provided. Place them there lying down in a vertical direction.

When eating with hands, the unbroken rule is to wash your hands prior to eating and when you have finished your meal. This makes it easier to indicate. Simply request either a bowl of water or napkins to clean your hands, and the server will know you have finished your meal.

In all instances, a gentle wave or catching the eye of the server will bring the server to your table, and you can let them know you have finished your meal and could you have the bill please.

How to Handle a Drunk Guest

The venue is irrelevant. As a host, you must take the responsibility of your guests' safety. You need to ensure that your guests arrive safely for your event and arrive safely back to their home at the end of the event. We all recall being at an event and, perhaps due to bad weather, a guest had not arrived. Phone calls were made to them to confirm their safety. The same practice applies to the ending of the event. If the weather is unwelcoming for whatever reason, it is good etiquette when you get home to send a text or make a call to the hosts to let them know you arrived safely. The same courtesy and regard for safety must be applied when handling a drunk guest.

At the beginning of festivities, you could announce in a charming and diplomatic manner that you wish everyone a delightful evening and request that they keep an eye on you in case you become too cheerful and inebriated, as they must stop you from drinking any more. The message, although not directed at any one person, is clear: It applies to everyone. Mention the fact that if they cannot drive home, you have made a bed up for them to stay overnight and it will not be an imposition at all.

When alcohol is involved, as a host we do need to exert a sense of responsibility, and at times potentially difficult decisions need to be made. You will be serving alcohol at your function, and to ensure no one is totally inebriated and incapacitated, you must take measures to prevent that from happening. "Prevention is better than cure," the elders of history have repeated to us over and over. If you can see there are signs of someone who is drinking excessively or who cannot handle their liquor, then you need to ensure that they are not given any more. Keep an eye on them and, if necessary, stay physically close to them. It is an unfortunate thing to happen, but as a host, it is your responsibility.

You can also close the bar at home an hour or two before the end of festivities and serve coffee and desserts or other snacks. This will give those who are inebriated time to sober up, and you can reassess their state.

If at the end of the evening, some guests cannot drive and do not want to stay with you, see if other guests are able to drive them home. Alternatively, they can leave their car at your place and get a taxi or allow you to drive them home. Bear in mind, taxis have no obligation to ensure your guest arrives inside their home safely.

As a final resort, you may have to have a designated driver ready to take guests home who need it. Safety is paramount for your guests.

This is the ultimate courtesy to others and is etiquette at its best, ensuring the safety of your guest.

Who Pays for the First Date or Business Meeting?

The first date could be the last date if this is not managed in a diplomatic manner that both parties find acceptable. It's the question that easily raises hotly debated answers. I know, I sound like a broken record, but consider where in the world you are, the situation and environment, and the prevailing etiquette there.

What are your options? The gentleman could pay on the first date. This would be easy enough, but then the lady may feel there is an obligation to return this with a subsequent meal, and it could be awkward if there is no desire to do so. The lady could pay, but the gentleman may feel uncomfortable. The third option is to pay for your own meals, and this way there are no expectations on either side, nor any sense of discomfort.

Now that you know the options, it's time to plan how best one can manage the situation so there is no awkwardness when the bill arrives. Establishing clarity and expectations at the onset are essential and important. It would be good etiquette when inviting the other party to indicate, "I would like to invite you for a meal or coffee." That would normally suffice, as inviting is a strong indication you are paying. However, in North America, it is best to add, "It is my treat." This way it is abundantly clear the person inviting is paying. The same practice would apply if you are going to expect each party to pay for themselves. You would say we are going Dutch or AA to indicate that you are splitting the bill. This way you avoid awkwardness when the bill arrives.

Other considerations must include what generations are involved. Generational approaches are different when dealing with splitting the bill or going Dutch. It is more the norm than the exception with millennials and generations thereafter, while for Generation X and before it is not that common.

In my experience over the years and in different countries, business settings are quite clear. If you invite the other party for lunch or dinner, you pay. There is no gray area here.

BUSINESS ETIQUETTE

IN THIS SECTION, we step into the world of business and delve into understanding the machinations and correct procedures when meeting, gifting, introducing in a business situation, and following up. You will gain insights into how to introduce yourself apart from shaking hands, how to deal with awkward situations, when to stand up or not, and more. This section will arm you with greater confidence when interacting on a business level. You will be more aware of the unwritten rules of etiquette and protocols for success in the global world of commerce and recognize how a minor step or shake can change the mood or the outcome of a meeting.

From the times of the ancient Silk Road, where long and winding caravans of camels trekked across blazing deserts, mountainous regions, and plains, the reward was commerce. The Venetians and their firm defense and hold on the Dalmatian coast was all for the sake of commerce. Spices from Malacca delivered by the Dutch and tea by the famous tea clippers all fed into commerce. With each portion of history, emissaries and ambassadors schooled in the arts of negotiation, languages, and etiquette made the difference. The faces change, the products may be microchips, smartphones, and oil, but the principles remain. Business is important and business etiquette more so. You are the next generation. By taking in this section, you will learn to tread wisely and fruitfully like your predecessors.

Five Etiquette Factors to Consider When Traveling Abroad

Technology has connected continents in ways that few could imagine a few years ago. I would even dare to say that ten years after this book has been published, what we know today will have been replaced by even more efficient, safer, and faster ways of connecting people together. It's true that the Internet, social media platforms, Google, Microsoft, and others have given all of us options for seeing and talking to others without the immediate need to meet. Meeting in person could well be delayed, but it will come one day. When that day comes, and it will, you need to be prepared to travel. Here are five factors to consider when planning your business travel abroad.

You will always meet someone during your business travels. The purpose of your meeting is to either sign, investigate, close a deal, or grow your business. Meeting and greeting people will be expected, so ensure you know the correct etiquette to do so, especially with cultures different from your own. Know how to correctly greet others in the country you are visiting. You may be required to shake hands, bow, or nod; whatever the case, be prepared.

Be prepared to function without internet. Countries differ in their internet connectivity, so it is very possible that the country you will be visiting does not have the level you are used to or expect. Using the new digital business cards are certainly useful and helpful, but they operate best with connectivity. In countries where they use the classic paper business card, especially in Asia, there is even a ceremony of handing one's card to another. The business card is held with both hands with the thumb and forefinger on either side of the card, each holding one corner. One cannot just hand it over in a simple flick of the wrist. To do so is a highly rude gesture to the receiver. So, it is important to always have paper business cards and to become acquainted with the business etiquette where you will be.

Always address people with respect. Countries like Japan address people in accordance with their seniority, position, title, and age. When addressing your counterpart, depending on where you are travelling to, ensure to use the correct words that show the appropriate respect for their position. The Middle East, Asia, and parts of Europe are not as casual as North America when addressing one another. In North America, unless you are a medical doctor, it is not common for people to address you as doctor, even though you may hold a doctorate degree. In Europe and Asia though, you are addressed according to your title and even profession at times. I cannot stress how important it is to address people with respect, and if you do make a mistake, you may not be even aware of it.

Giving gifts is quite common when visiting business associates in other countries. Take time to understand what gifts are appropriate, including the color, number, type, and value of gifts to consider and how you wrap them. An inappropriate gift can cause embarrassment and affect the outcome of your travel. In many countries, do not give any object with a sharp edge, as it is symbolic of cutting off friendships.

You will be wined and dined, so be prepared. If you don't know how to eat with your hands or how to use chopsticks, then learn. If you are not comfortable using a knife and fork, then become comfortable. As a modern-day businessperson and with the access to the Internet, there is no excuse for not being prepared.

Place yourself in the position of the host, expecting a business mission to arrive to your country and company. If the entire mission is *au fait* with your country's etiquette, how would you feel? Certainly more at ease, so be prepared and leave a lasting positive impression.

Dress Code for Business Travel Abroad

The world is changing in attitudes, living style, values, and most definitely dress code. It used to be unthinkable that anyone in a professional capacity would be seen in public without a jacket and a tie. Today it is quite common in North America for the attire to be an open neck shirt and jacket sans tie. Yet in Hong Kong, Korea, and Japan, it would be unthinkable to wear a jacket without a tie! The key is to dress respectfully, not only for the business colleagues you are visiting, but also for the country and, above all, yourself.

When you next visit London, go to Jermyn Street and be inspired by a statue of Beau Brummell. He is considered the innovator of the business suit that men wear today across the globe. For many men, one suit (preferably dark blue), a combination of different colored pants (perhaps black, gray and tan), a few white and light blue button-up shirts, and some polo shirts will suffice for any major business meetings. Have a tie, a good leather belt, and quality shoes as well.

For ladies, conservative wear is preferable, as the dress code for women can vary when visiting many countries. A standard suit with pants or skirt is highly recommended (dark blue preferred) and all the standard accessories as well. In the worst-case scenario, if your clothing is not appropriate, then a shopping spree is required when you can. You should try to outfit yourself in advance so you don't stand out like a sore thumb. One would not want your dress to be the main topic, diverting attention from the business at hand.

If your culture requires a headdress, like a yarmulke or kippah for Jewish men, headscarf, turban like the Sikhs, or another type, then by all means do wear it. But please, you must be aware that regulations and laws differ from country to country when pertaining to the wearing of certain headdress in public. You will very quickly realize when travelling that dress codes are vastly different country to country and even region to region within a country.

What may be acceptable dress in your country might be totally unsuitable in another. If you are not sure, then be prudent and dress more conservatively. When you are abroad and you have free time, it is only natural that you may want to take advantage of this opportunity and see the sights. Remember that there are dress codes for entering certain sites. In Rome, if you are visiting St. Peter's, Basilica, women cannot enter if they expose too much of their body, like shoulders and midriff. In such cases, you are required to cover yourself. If you don't have other clothing, the authorities at these venues may give you a blanket to cover yourself. Similarly, when entering a mosque, like the Hagia Sophia in Istanbul, or a synagogue, conservative clothing must be worn. If you take a tour of the Jewish quarter in Venice, you must wear a yarmulke or head covering.

Dress code applies equally to men as it does for women. In Jordan for example, men should wear long trousers and a shirt. T-shirts are tolerated, but a button-down shirt is perfect. Shorts must be at least knee-length. There are some unfamiliar dress codes that appear strange to outsiders. When driving in Spain, you cannot wear sandals. It is an offense. In many Caribbean countries, like Barbados, you cannot wear camouflage clothing unless you are in the military.

Not that you would want to wear high heels from a comfort standpoint when going to visit the Acropolis in Greece, but it is also not permitted to protect the site. Harrods in London will not allow you into the store if your clothing is considered inappropriate or has offensive writing on it.

The list can go on and on, and all it does is give further evidence that dress codes matter when travelling abroad for business or pleasure. Respect the dress wear etiquette of the country you are visiting.

The Amicable Way of a Business Handshake

The origins of the handshake are murky. There is evidence though that the handshake has been in use for centuries. A ninth century BCE relief of a handshake by the Assyrian king Shalmaneser and a Babylonian ruler is one of the earliest depictions found of a handshake. Since then, handshakes have been around and in constant use.

The handshake movement can be dissected into several parts. The position of your hand when shaking, where your eyes are looking, the intensity of your grip, the number of times you shake hands, and when both parties end the handshake. The etiquette for these details differs from culture to culture.

In North America and Western Europe, a good handshake begins from the elbow, not the shoulder. The wrist and the forearm remain firm. It's not good form to have the back of your hand facing the sky, as if you are trying to stress your dominant character. Neither should your palm be facing the sky with the other party's hand on top, as that portrays a weak character. The hand should be in a parallel position to the sky and ground. This is the optimal position one should maintain, and it shows a firm and fair posture. The handshake should be firm, but not pain-inducing. That serves no purpose apart from creating a negative opinion. You should look at the other person's eyes when you shake hands.

In Asian countries like Japan, China, Korea, and India, which makes up approximately 40 percent of the world's population, the handshake is quite gentle and they do not look you in the eye, as that is considered rude and bad etiquette. For many countries, a short handshake is preferable for business meetings, no more than two shakes and a clear-cut separation of the hands, sometimes referred to as a pump. In Asia, the handshake is slightly longer, while in South America, it can be much longer, say four to five pumps.

Knowing that you are going to be shaking hands in business, it is good form to wash your hands and ensure that they are not clammy or sticky. Having clean hands is polite.

When and How Should You Bow?

When introducing yourself to others, there are several ways to do that (page 34). You can shake hands, hold your two palms together with the tips of your fingers pointing towards the sky, nod your head, bow, or even a combination of the options. Certainly in business meetings, getting it right the first time is an asset and reflects that you have done your homework in advance.

Why do people bow? Bowing is used to show respect, gratitude, appreciation, or even to indicate goodbye. We have seen Asian CEOs and government ministers bow in public when offering an apology to the public and others. Before training for martial arts, the students and sensei bow to one another. People bow when saying goodbye to one another; it is the same as them waving their hands indicating they are leaving. Even at the saddest of moments in life upon the passing of a friend or relative, when you want to express sympathy, a bow is very much appreciated and appropriate.

Bowing is entrenched in Asian culture and not seen as a subservient movement, in fact quite the opposite.

Can you bow and shake hands at the same time? You could, but its best to do one at a time. A word of caution: Make sure both parties will either shake hands or bow and not the opposite to one another. After bowing, you can shake hands.

Westerners prefer to shake hands, so it can be a common occurrence in travels to not know when to shake hands or bow. A simple rule to follow is watch and follow the actions taken by the host. By doing so, your host can also assist in preventing an embarrassing moment from occurring. Another clue to look for is that if someone is going to bow, they will generally stop a short distance away from you, then bow. After the bow, they will continue walking toward you, and then, if you wish, you can shake hands as well.

Now that you have an idea of when to bow and you know the different reasons as to why you should bow, let's look at how to bow. Keep your neck and back straight when bowing and your eyes looking downward. If you look at the other person when bowing, it is a sign of aggression. Also, you should hold your hands to your side or in front of you. It is preferred that women bow with their fingertips touching or hands clasped in front of them. Always face the person you are bowing to, squarely and not too close, otherwise you could bang your heads.

The lower you bow, the greater the respect you are offering. A general fifteen-degree bow is standard, and a forty-five degree bow is big. The number of times you bow is important too. A singular bow is used for people you are greeting. If the people are deceased, then two to three bows are required. Certainly, you should make three bows when going to a temple.

Superb! You have perhaps not mastered the art of bowing, but at least you are more familiar with the bowing etiquette. If you are going to do anything, do it well.

How to Introduce Yourself in a New Work Environment

To bow, shake hands, or nod is probably the first thing going through your mind, and you would not be wrong. Whenever people know there will be a new person, it always arouses a sense of different emotions. There is interest, curiosity, expectations, and even a high level of anticipation.

Naturally, there will be the perfunctory array and battery of questions. Where are you from? What do you do? What do your parents do? Are they still alive? How many siblings do you have? And you should be able to reply with those very well rehearsed answers.

In a business environment, you represent change, and change is hard for people to accept, whether it is good or bad. Everyone has a unique perspective, and you must be aware of that. You need to be able to assess who sees you as an ally and those who see you as a threat. One way to figure it out is to think about who is asking you the most questions. Who is asking the questions relating to your past work experience more? Who is asking you personal questions? At least you can decipher from the frequency and type of questions who the questioner is. You, in turn, when the opportunity arises, can also ask questions and openly assess their answers. By answering your questions, they are revealing themselves.

Strategically, that is what you need to do when entering an unfamiliar environment. To give your best impression to others, your introduction should consider who you are talking to, the formality of the situation, and if it is during or after working hours. You should customize your introduction and there should be three clear sections. Begin with the present: who you are, where you will be working, and what you will be doing in your position at the company. Then spend some time on what you did before joining, a little about your past. And finally, end it with your expectations of work, hope for growth, and happiness about joining this team. The tone should not be aggressive, aloof, timid, or fearful, but it should express balance and confidence. This way the principles of self respect, courtesy for others, and grace are all in line with the self-etiquette you practice.

Corporate Gift Etiquette

Exchanging gifts is quite natural, and many of us give and receive gifts during the festive holiday season. Gifts require deep thought, as they send a message to the recipient of the gift. If it is a corporate gift, then greater importance is attached not only about the message but the intention. There are external gifts to clients and suppliers and internal gifts to colleagues and staff.

Giving gifts to staff is easier, as it can come in the form of a monetary bonus that is given to all staff but in varying amounts. Another form can be during the staff holiday party or another special time of the year, like summer or spring.

However, when sending external gifts, it is important that the business gift offered is not perceived in any manner whatsoever as a potential bribe, or described in a more diplomatic way, a facilitating fee. Budget is always a consideration, not so much about how much you are going to spend on the gift, but rather the limit of the value of the gift that the recipient can accept. Over-the-limit gifts might be expensive watches, season tickets to sport matches and, in some cases, the full tuition costs of sending the person's child to university. Gifts of such high value can be questioned.

The true cost is the perception of motivation and the possible trouble your gift can cause the recipient with their company and authorities because of that perception. If you are not sure about the value, ask your contacts at the company if there are limits. Oftentimes, the government of the country also sets limits.

In North America and Europe, corporate gift receiving is a very delicate affair, so offering branded company gifts is balanced and reduces any possible misconception about the intention. It is quite normal when high-ranked visitors go to visit a company that they will receive gifts from the company, and the visitors themselves also offer a gift.

In Asia, it is expected that when going with a delegation on a trade visit, gifts will be exchanged. If you are hosting a tour for Asian counterparts, ensure your have gifts prepared for everyone, which includes a more generous gift for the head and a standard gift for the other members. If the recipients are Japanese, ensure your packaging is superb and without a crinkle, as they take their packing very seriously.

Another consideration when giving gifts is the type of gift and to whom you are giving gifts. Any gifts with a sharp edge means cutting of friendship and ties, and Italians don't like receiving those gifts. A strong suggestion would be to research international customs in advance and etiquette about gift giving. If you do business internationally, your clients or partners may have different expectations when it comes to the etiquette of gift giving. Also, if you are going during a particular holiday time, understand and know what traditional gifts are given during that period, like Chinese New Year, Christmas, or Thanksgiving.

Whatever the reason, giving gifts is a sign of one's appreciation for the other person who is receiving the gift. It symbolizes and sends a message. Apply the correct etiquette to send the right message.

How to Handle Awkward Questions at Your Initial Meeting

Business meetings can be compared to small tributaries flowing that eventually join into one big river. The purpose of the meeting is to see if there is good flow in one direction. The river would be representative of a successful business venture together. The tributaries are to find out about you, the business, and a possible future alignment with the two companies.

The business questions can be easily answered, but the chances are they know about your company in advance and the fact that they are meeting suggests they do see a potential future. The gaping question is the soft power, the people power: You are the unknown factor that they want to assess. It's all part of the introduction etiquette and how well you acquit yourself.

The perfunctory questions may begin with innocent questions about your visit if you are in a foreign country. Is it your first time visiting the country? When were you last in the country? If you are in your own country or city, the questions may pertain to something local. These are the warm-up questions, then the barrage will commence. Sometimes the questions asked are to assess your reaction: Do you get irritated easily, become anxious, show you are upset, or remain calm and unperturbed? The questions are asked to get a reaction from you. The trick is to know when a question is poised to elicit a reaction.

Consider questions about what your parents do for a living, your marriage status, your birthplace, or the car you drive. These questions may appear very personal and unrelated to the business at hand. That is certainly true in the Western Europe and North American context, but in other parts of the world, these are standard questions and not considered personal at all. In fact, by not asking these questions, you might feel they have no interest in you at all! In Asian countries like India, China, Thailand, and Singapore, these are very standard. The purpose of these questions is to know about you, your background, your stability, and your status and position in life.

On the other hand, if you asked someone from the United States who they voted for in the last election, you might get a very heated or irritated response. Politics is certainly one of the taboo topics of conversation for initial meetings (page 55), and the use of such topics could be a way to get you to react or it could be an etiquette faux pas.

The possible questions asked of you are not always intended to make you feel negatively. If you can mentally prepare yourself for such questions, you have done very well to be open and flexible. You are, after all, very possibly in another part of the world where etiquette and norms differ.

How to Offer Your Contact Information

Contact information in today's age is a valuable resource. Network meetings, charitable clubs, business associations, and other clubs all have the two main objectives. One is to meet people, and the second is to share interests, whether it is a hobby, sport, or purely business.

I have shared the many ways one can share information with others, as well as the etiquette and protocol one should use. The business card is still used quite broadly, although a growing number are using electronic scan cards now. Another way of sharing is to give your phone to others. At times, I have seen people offer their phone to those from whom they want their contact information. It is easier for that person to type in the information on the phone directly. How you exchange the contact information is the easy part. Deciding whom to share it with is the part I would like to address now. In terms of etiquette, be careful who you ask for contact information.

In Asia, especially China, Japan, and Korea, they use systems called guanxi, wa, and inhwa, respectively. These are similar in nature and the principle where relationships are of the utmost importance. These terms are used to describe a person's social network of business and personal relationships based on loyalty, harmony, hierarchy, and consensus principles.

For example, imagine you are visiting a number of countries in Asia and you do not know anyone there. You have asked your U.S. friend, who lived in Hong Kong before, if he can introduce you to anyone in Hong Kong. Your friendship is important to him, so he introduces you to his friend based in Hong Kong. You are wined and dined by others in Hong Kong because of your friend's introduction. You are dined and welcomed, not because you are special, but your friend's relationship with you is special and his friends respect him, so they are looking after you. To pay respect to your friend in the United States, your Hong Kong hosts look after you extremely well and for no other reason.

Guanxi is very different from the Western circle of influence of acquaintance, associate, and friend. You are either in the circle or not in Asia. Now here comes the tricky part. Your newly found host invites you to a business dinner and there he introduces you to others. Coming from North America, you find it only normal practice to share your contact details with others and receive contact details in return. That is the problem.

In this instance, should anyone want to have your contact details, you should ask them politely to contact your host, unless your host initially says it is no problem to share your details with one another. If that permission is not granted, then do not give your information unless you wish to break a bond. It also applies when you want the information of someone; it is best you ask your host for it.

In conversation, you can say to the other person, "I will get your information from my host." If you go directly ignoring this protocol and get the information from the other person, you will be cutting off all your relationships with this newly acquired host that your friend arranged for you. Your friend in the United States will also have his relationship impaired with your current host because of your actions. Adhering to the correct etiquette is massively important. Knowing "who" to ask is the true "how" to ask when it comes to exchanging contact information.

Dress Code for a Business Meeting

There are several considerations to make before deciding on a rigid rule about wearing a shirt, tie, and suit to all business meetings. It is important for many reasons that one dresses appropriately for business meetings. Given the serious nature of such meetings, your dress code becomes a representation of that gravitas.

Who you meet and the industry they are in is one factor to consider. If you are meeting people in the information technology (IT) industry, it is much more casual. It is widely known, reported on, and photographed that IT business meetings are more casual and can mean jeans, t-shirts, and sneakers instead of the stodgy button-up shirts and ties. They opt more for the loose and casual appearance, but that does not belie the seriousness of the meeting.

Where and what time of the year the meeting takes place is another consideration. If you are going to Hong Kong in July, the average temperature for the month is about 30 degrees Celsius (86 degrees Fahrenheit), which is hot as it is, but add the typical local humidity, and that makes it decidedly toasty. However, the standard business attire in Hong Kong is jacket and tie. That is the norm and that is what is expected when you have business meetings there. Anything less and you could be considered underdressed and displaying poor etiquette.

The nature of the business meeting may allow some latitude in dress expectations. In general, most meetings of a serious nature will require more formal business wear in the form of suits and ties. Another consideration is what is the environment of the city and their norm. We mentioned Hong Kong where it is suit and tie despite the weather. In Canada, on the East Coast in Toronto, there is more of a tendency to wear suits and ties if you are in the legal, financial, and professional circles, whereas on the West Coast of Canada in Vancouver, there is a more casual approach. If people wear a jacket, they will not necessarily wear the tie.

Whatever you do decide to wear, ensure it is clean, perhaps not necessarily ironed, although that would be a bonus. The last thing you want is to be like a fish out of water in the dress sense: Everyone is wearing t-shirts and jeans and you are wearing a three-piece suit. It not only looks odd, but you are in essence not following their etiquette and protocol.

Remember, where the meeting is being held, the industry involved, when it is being held, who you are meeting, and the nature of the meeting will be definite guidelines to help you navigate the dress code.

Conduct at a Conference or Trade Show

Conferences and trade shows are notorious for being like speed dating. You know time is limited and you want to see everything all at once, but you cannot, and you don't want to commit either. Commitment is more for speed dating, but for conferences and trade shows, the commitment is more about who should you spend more or less time with. I am going to use wine shows as the example here.

Having marched many kilometers across the hallways, passages, and presentation rooms of multiple wine shows across the globe, I know the importance of pacing yourself. If you do your best, you can hope to trudge yourself back to your hotel with multiple blisters, and at worst, it will be an absolute death crawl with your calves seizing up on you. Unbecoming conduct is not how you want to be remembered.

If you are the vendor, etiquette and manners are of prime importance because the main impression you leave with others will be you and secondly the wine. You understandably want to increase your customers and sales, so your welcoming manner when potential clients approach you is so important. A smile and a happy face are a good start. Remember to have your array of endless supplies of business cards to offer, and when offering them, do so in the respectable way by knowing your situation and environment (page 24).

Listen, respond, and be gracious to everyone you meet and know when to stop engaging. You may have others waiting to see or speak to you. People attending shows and conferences know time is scarce, so they will not be offended. Contact has been made with the person, and you can follow up with them later.

If you are the visitor to the show or conference, be clear with what you are looking for and advise the person or the booth that you are visiting of exactly what you need and ask if they can accommodate your business request. This way you don't waste their time or yours. It is not rude, but practical, and they will appreciate your candidness and good business practices.

Do ask and take contact details of the vendor. Because you have collected so many cards, you may forget the people related to the business card. My tip is to take a photo together to remind yourself and link the business card with the photo. Of course, ask permission before you take the photo and let them know why. They normally are intrigued that you thought of this.

Be clear, polite, respectful, and always assess those to whom you are speaking. Be mindful of time constraints, and after the show, send one email on the day of the show or the next day and then a week after the show to communicate with your new contact. Why one week? Normally, you or they have to travel back to their country, then there is the need to settle down and catch up. By waiting a week, you have both done so. If not, it's very possible your email will be lost in the deluge of emails that have backed up in your or their absence.

Follow those guidelines and I assure you no one can claim you are not following good business etiquette.

Cultural Sensitivity When Selecting a Restaurant

Every country has different values, norms, and expectations when it relates to dining, especially with others. The differences are reflected in their culture and etiquette. Awareness of the differences shows your client you are sensitive to their culture and enhances your relationship.

Almost every major city in the world has a vast range of international cuisines to select from when deciding to enjoy a meal with a client. Whether you are hosting locally or internationally, the same principles apply.

Your choice is reflective of your level of sophistication, awareness, and respect for your guest. The quality of food matters in many cultures. For certain cultures, the alcohol is more important than the food, whereas the Spanish, French, and Italians are very particular about the food served and the ambience. Wine and food often dominate the conversation with people from Europe, certainly during the early part of the evening. Your lack of or your in-depth knowledge of food and wine will be on display, so be prepared.

Consider food restrictions that are specific to a particular group, such as people of the Jewish or Muslim faith. Both groups do not eat pork, and the Jewish faith has many other restrictions, like any shellfish is not permitted and only fish that have fins and scales are allowed. Muslim meats have to be halal, which means they must be "permitted" meats where the animal was killed in a certain way. Muslims will only eat at restaurants that serve such meats. If you are not sure, ask the restaurant if their meats are halal or not. If your guest is of the Hindu faith, they do not eat beef.

Certain restaurants allow both males and females to eat together, while some cultures do not permit that, mainly Arabic countries, and one should be aware of that when selecting the restaurant. Another consideration is the seating arrangement you require. Does the restaurant have the space to accommodate any specific style or arrangement you need? For example, if a round table is required, ensure one is available.

In some cultures, alcohol is not permitted at all, while in others it is the standard way to opening the path to friendship and creating a more relaxing environment. In China, be prepared to be toasted by every single person individually seated at your table if you are the guest of honor. This method of toasting is similar in Korea. If your guests are very strict about alcohol, then you should perhaps not choose a restaurant that serves alcohol on their premises.

During the meal, cultures differ with their conversation style. With the French, they will appreciate your commenting about how wonderful the food is, then after the meal you can discuss business. It is the reverse with the Germans: They will discuss business before the meal. The Japanese enjoy eating and drinking and, of course, singing after the meeting. Understanding the etiquette of each country may prove hard, but being aware is of great personal advantage to you.

Where to Sit for a Formal Business Dinner

Business dinners play many roles, and each party extracts certain information from the event. They observe, study, absorb, and then analyze later that evening. Don't be naïve thinking that it is just a dinner; it is so much more. Where you sit at such a dinner can make all the difference.

In most instances in North America and Western Europe, the dinner tables are rectangular in shape. The seating arrangements for tables that have this shape are quite simple. The host would sit at the head of the table and the guests would then be seated on the sides of the table. The seating order would place the guest of honor on the right side of the host, and if the guest has a partner, they would be seated on the left side of the host. If there are two hosts, the other host would sit at the end of the table that was unoccupied so at either ends of the table there would be a host. The other guests would be seated alongside the guests of honor, frequently seated according to rank and position. The next criteria would be a male then a female guest alternately. The third criteria would be for the guests to be seated next to a member of the other company, so no two members of the same company are seated together.

How do you know where to sit though? If the dinner is very formal, then most likely there will be a place setting with your name on it. If there are no place settings, then it would be polite to await seating instructions from the host. As a reminder for gentlemen, should you have ladies seated on either side of you, it would be good etiquette to ask the ladies if you could seat them.

If the table is circular, which is often the case in Asia and certainly China for formal business dinner settings, then seating arrangements are slightly different. The host will always face the entrance to the restaurant or entrance to the room if a private room was booked. The host will never have their back facing the entrance, as they cannot see who is leaving and entering the room. The guest of honor will sit on the right of the host and the next guest of honor would sit on their left side. As the table is circular, should there be another host for the evening, they would sit with their back facing the entrance. In this position, both of the hosts can see one another, and in this way they can take care of their guests.

As a guest to a formal business dinner, you must conduct yourself in manner that is expected of your stature and position. Etiquette strongly suggests that you dress appropriately as well.

Topics to Avoid at a Business Dinner

Apart from avoiding the universal trilogy of taboo topics (money, religion, and politics) at any meal, you need to also take the cue from the host at the business dinner. If you can, try to follow, expand, and then divert the dinner conversation with compelling and interesting topics that can involve everyone.

Should it appear that your host would like to discuss a particular topic and you are comfortable with it, then engage. The purpose of the meeting might be to explore your thoughts about a particular or potential business opportunity. Feel free to discuss, but always show restraint. If you are not comfortable, find diplomatic ways to avoid the question without appearing devious. Again, consider the situation and environment you are in when answering or discussing anything.

Some of the main discussion rules are never to gossip or talk ill of any person or body. When you indulge in that type of conversation, you lower your self-esteem, and if you were to do that, the host may think that on another occasion you may also speak about them behind their back. Always be cognizant of how you behave. The host will believe that your behavior in his presence reflects the way you will behave in his absence. Apply caution when you speak and how you react.

In certain countries, it is impolite to discuss the health and appearance of others at the dinner table until the person mentions the topic themselves. Depending on the makeup of the guests, if you decide to tell a joke, ensure that all of your guests speak English well if you are going to say your joke in English. If they don't, it's possible they will not understand and might think you are talking about them or joking at their expense. In France, don't ask people what they do for a living or ask about their personal life until they bring it up. If you bring it up, that is poor etiquette. Other areas one should be careful of are topics on poverty, pollution, education, and governance. There are so many safe and enjoyable topics to explore, like sports, interests, movies, and travel experiences. When the evening moves on and you can assess the mood and flexibility, then you can slowly expand your scope of conversation. Let common sense prevail when discussing topics at a business dinner.

Cutlery Use During a Business Meal

In Africa, there is a proverb that says, "Monkeys place by size." The meaning is taken from nature where, in Africa, you will never see a big baboon or gorilla mingling with a small monkey. In the context of dining, groups and individuals who have a certain decorum and etiquette wish nothing less than to have those around them to also have this same sense of propriety. This is especially true for those who gather for business dinners at high-end restaurants.

Imagine you are about to have a meal at any one of these restaurants: Restaurant Guy Savoy in Paris, Restaurant de l'Hôtel de Ville in Crissier, Switzerland, or The Ritz Restaurant in the Ritz hotel in London. How do you use your cutlery? In a single phrase, "Begin from the outside and work inward." Forks are placed on the left-hand side of the main plate below your bread plate and bread knife. On the right-hand side of your plate are your knives, soup spoons, and glasses for wine and water. Dessert cutlery is placed above the plate. Many of you are remarkably familiar with the cutlery and how to use them. If not, then I suggest you do become familiar (page 93). Your fellow diners may not comment, but they will observe and make their own assessments.

Let's explore the use of cutlery in other countries. You might be invited to the Kitcho Arashiyama in Kyoto, Cai Yi Xuan in Beijing, Mingles in Seoul, or another high-end Asian restaurant, and the cutlery there consists of chopsticks. There is no working from out to in here. There will most likely be two sets of chopsticks, one for eating and the other for serving, as well as a soup spoon for eating and another for serving. Refer to the dining section for more tips on what you should and should not do when dining Asian style (page 90). You may also be unfamiliar with the hot towel they give you, which comes alive when they pour hot water onto the towelette. It is called an "oshibori" and comes in many forms. When in doubt, my suggestion is to follow your host's lead and see how they use the utensils and towels provided. This way, by waiting, you are showing respect to the host, and this also will not embarrass the host.

If you are in India, Ethiopia, the Middle East, and other parts of Africa, you may be treated to special high-end restaurant where you use your hands (page 92). If the last time you ate with your hands regularly was the time you were learning to speak, it would be quite unfamiliar and possibly feel awkward as well. When eating with your hands, wash them first and only eat with your right hand. Never bring your head to your hand, but your hand with the food towards your mouth.

Eat with your mouth closed, and never talk with food in your mouth. When putting food into your mouth, avoid putting your fingers in as well. Again, if you are not sure, watch your host.

If you do make a mistake, don't be overly conscious of other guests, as they may not notice. They may be concentrating on the food, conversation, and how to use their own cutlery too. Often, like you, the other guests may be a bit lost as to how to eat correctly. Concentrate on your own etiquette and let others worry about their behavior.

Cutlery, as you have discovered, is not only the knife and fork!

Napkin Placement When Leaving the Table

When at a business meeting, you want to squeeze in every precious moment you have with your client or guest and avoid leaving the table. Sometimes nature calls though and you have no choice, or there may be other extenuating circumstances that require you leave the table momentarily. It is at this time that you have to leave your napkin, that is currently on your thigh, somewhere. The question is where?

You have three choices, and only one is correct etiquette. You could place it on the seat of the chair where you were sitting. This may appear the best place because, if your napkin is soiled with the flavorful marinara sauce from the pasta, no one will see it if you place it on the seat. The only problem is that the seat is not a very clean place, and if the napkin is soiled it may leave stains on the chair. When sitting down again, any dirt or sauce will be transferred onto your clothes. So that is not the correct option.

The other option would be to hang the napkin like a flag on the upright portion of the chair. Once again, the soiled napkin will be seen by all the other guests. Not a very appetizing sight, so rule this option out.

The third and final option is to place the napkin on the table. You could place it on the right-hand side of the plate, but then some servers may interpret that as you have finished your meal and take your plate away. When you come back, not only is your napkin is not there, but your dinner has disappeared as well.

Think of your table setting as a "BMW." The "B" represents the bread on the left side of the "M." The letter "M" represents the meal, and the "W" refers to the wine on the right side of the main meal. It is simplistic, but it does help those that seem intimidated by table settings. With the mystery of the napkin, we will use the "LLL" abbreviation. This means "Leave Loose on the Left." The napkin should be left loosely on the left side of the main plate. The loosely means do not wrap your napkin back into shape, but place it loosely in a way so no stains are visible for the other guests. Some overly enthusiastic and inexperienced server seeing your napkin carefully wrapped back into shape may take your dish thinking you have finished your meal.

A failsafe way is to ask your fellow guest to ensure the waiter does not take your meal before you return. One final tip: If you happen to drop your napkin, do not pick it up and put it back onto your thigh. Please request a new one, as a dirty napkin is not hygienic.

What to Do When Food Gets Stuck in the Teeth

I recall a particular trip to a rather famous area in northeast China. After visiting a winery that produced ice wine, the owner wanted to honor me with a meal. There were several dishes, and one of them was a fish dish. As was common in that part of the world, the fish served was not filleted. As fate would have it, while enjoying the flavorful meal, I managed to chomp down on a fishbone. It lodged right into my upper left gum. I had hoped that I would be able to muster along and put on a brave face during lunch.

In this case, retreat was the better part of valor, and I excused myself from the table and went to the washroom. There, despite the help of a mirror, I was still unable to pull out the fish bone. Eventually, I had to call upon my assistant to help me, and we were successful after a few attempts.

Should you ever get any food stuck in between your teeth, I suggest if it is uncomfortable, excuse yourself from the table. Ask for a toothpick or floss at the restaurant reception or from the manager, then go to the washroom. Do not use your fingernail or toothpick to dig at your tooth while seated at the table. If you can bear it, then wait until after the meal and take care of the irritant back at your hotel room.

I have seen people use the edge of a business card, which they have just received, to try and jiggle the stuck piece out of their mouth. The preferred way is to leave the table. If you are unable to do so for whatever reason and you must get the piece removed, then cover your mouth with the one free hand and do your best. It would be obvious what you are doing and not a pretty sight for your other guests. Again, it depends on the situation and environment.

If you happen to see another guest, who has perhaps a piece of spinach or another particle stuck in between their teeth and they unaware of it, you should let them know.

At the appropriate time when you have their attention and others are not watching, discreetly use your finger and point at your own mouth, perhaps tapping on your tooth, and they will understand your meaning. Whenever I have done this, I have always had a favorable and appreciative response. I know that if I had something stuck in my mouth or on my teeth, I would appreciate someone telling me rather than smiling in photos with something spoiling my smile.

Business Dinner Expense Limits

Before one can charge recklessly like a bull in a china shop claiming that a massive dinner bill is outrageous and shameful, one must exercise a balanced and measured response to defining expensive first.

The definition of expensive is relative. It is subjective, not objective. The reason for the dinner must be placed into the equation to calculate if it is indeed too expensive or not. The type of dinner, what is being ordered, when it is being eaten, if it is during a festive period or a marginally slower period, and how many people are attending the meal are all inclusive in the equation.

Can spending an obscene amount of money on a dinner be considered poor etiquette? It's not a simple question, as it could be answered truthfully as yes and with equal justification as no. To establish a framework for this scenario, we can use this example. Dinner is for ten people during a non-festive season of the year. The purpose is to celebrate the retirement of the owner of the business, who sold his enormously successful company to his former workers, now the new owners collectively. The business was sold for twenty million U.S. dollars after forty years.

In this instance, a lavish ten-course meal was arranged, the finest wines were drunk, and the best seafood and meats were offered. The venue was held at a high-end restaurant in a private room. The final bill came out to twenty thousand U.S. dollars, including a 20 percent tip for service. By many accounts, that would be an exceedingly large sum, perhaps even "over the top." Given the financial numbers of the business and the per person cost, however, it might seem reasonable to the person who paid the bill.

In keeping with what is culturally acceptable and good etiquette, one should certainly consider all of the factors mentioned and also the guests who are attending the dinner. In the example given, it was a transition of a very successful business, but had it been a new venture with a modest agreement sale for less than fifty thousand U.S.

dollars, then that might have been seen as excessive.

The amount that one can spend is without limit, as that depends on one's financial largess. The amount one should spend is more important and requires that all factors be placed into the equation. It's all relative, and this is a gray area you may well come across. Only you can decide in this case.

What to Do When You Hate the Expensive Meal Ordered in Your Honor

Simply put, you say nothing. Eat it and give thanks would be my suggestion. The only exemption would be legitimate dietary reasons you may have. Your host should know this in advance though, so don't try and fool them if you don't have any. Chances are your host already inquired before ordering the dish. Is it poor etiquette to say no to the dish? Yes, it would be poor etiquette in my opinion, but the final decision I leave to you.

It could be frog legs in France, or phoenix claws (chicken feet) in China, or haggis in Scotland. One may even have a particular dislike for caviar served in Hungary or deep-fried sheep eyeballs in Saudi Arabia. Whatever the dish and your dislike, your host's only intention is to honor you. As such, they have ordered an expensive dish. You may not particularly like it, but be graceful about the meaningful intention and enjoy it.

I had such an incident happen to me a few years ago. We had concluded a remarkably successful business transaction, and the host wanted to invite me to a special meal. I was not sure what they would offer, but knowing about the "losing face" phenomena for my host, I knew I would eat whatever they placed in front of me. They asked me if I preferred to have the ingredient in a stew or fried? I opted for fried, and it was a wise choice. When the dish came out, it was a huge deep-fried local brown snake!

I do eat everything and have no restrictions, but snake is not normal fare for me, and it is not a meal I would ever choose on my own. I had no qualms and ate the food placed on my plate. If it really is unpalatable, then at least take a small bite and leave the rest. If asked, say that you have tried a few bites and although it is not to your taste, you do like the other dishes. At least you did try and did not immediately say no at the beginning. Neither party will lose face and their reputations remain intact.

No matter how much you liked or disliked the dish, be gracious because you can be assured that your host will ask if you enjoyed the meal. A balanced response would be to highlight the entire meal and other dishes, and then allude to the dish they served as the main meal. You might say it was an experience to taste it and once in your lifetime is enough, otherwise next time you may get it again. Your sacrificial approach has saved your host's face, and your stature will have increased in value. It's their etiquette to honor you in this way.

Lawyer Tip: Ordering Wine for a Potential Client

Lawyers carry a certain notoriety with their profession. Some see them as 24/7 walking invoice machines that charge you for every single word they utter to you or hear from you. Their charges are based on six-minute intervals or thereabout, so can others be faulted for the jaded impression? There are those who see them as the defenders of the scales of justice, be it civil or criminal. Either way, it will cost you, and dearly.

If you are a lawyer, you probably already know that to most people, lawyers mean expenses. People have different perspectives of you: a savior in a divorce case, an executor of an estate, or even a defense lawyer. Whatever the role you are hired to perform, your clients do not believe your services come cheap.

Lawyers, like any other business representatives, need clients. Clients are their raw material. No clients, no income. They need to quote and offer their skills, just like any other service. My old law professor from my student days once said, "Lawyers, accountants, and taxi drivers are the same. They take you from point A to point B. It's just the charge that is different."

Lawyers rightly enjoy the fruits of their labor, and some of that comes in the form of entertaining, which is an advantage when they are pursuing potential clients. Clients, when considering a lawyer, evaluate two main points first: Can the lawyer do the work, and what sort of relationship can I have with this lawyer? If the answer is favorable to those questions, then a third question comes into play: What is the cost? This is not entirely a moot point, but it does fall into the world of semi-irrelevance. If the answer is unfavorable to either of the first two questions asked, then the third point can be an important deal breaker or a tie breaker perhaps.

How does this relate to etiquette? Well, public perception is that the ranks of professionals, like lawyers, accountants, engineers, architects, and doctors, are all well acquainted with the nuances of etiquette, and as such, they should show this in their social dealings. With such high expectations already, knowing your etiquette is essential.

Regarding the cost of a bottle of wine, when the recipient is a potential client, buying a bottle of wine that costs more than a hundred dollars might give the wrong impression. This can apply to any profession, not just lawyers. The cost of the wine should be reasonable. Anything too high ignites a thought in the mind of the potential client: Their six-minute fee rate must be high!

If you are an existing client and your lawyer wishes to invite you for a meal or for you to attend their client functions, you must be a very good paying client. Enjoy your invitation; you earned it.

Either way, lawyers make good money, and that is not a crime or crucifix they should carry. They worked for it and earned it with their sacrifices and intellect, as do other professions. Despite the stereotypical, less-than-positive impression one might have of lawyers, they do serve their constructive role in society and do give back to society.

WHAT TO DO WHEN THE HOST ASKS YOU TO SING AND DANCE

You have just agreed to sign a mammoth business deal. The lawyers are preparing the paperwork tonight, and it will be signed tomorrow. You have been invited by the other party to celebrate tonight with a dinner that includes singing—karaoke to be precise—afterward. You hate singing, and dancing is a fate worse than being tortured with a thousand lashes. But for the sake of business, you will have to subject yourself to an evening of (possibly) self-humiliation. Are you prepared to do this? For the glory and success of your business venture, you feel you should. Does this sound familiar? Did it happen to you, or you have heard a similar tale?

It certainly is possible you heard or experienced such tales if you have either traveled to Asia or done business there. That's because in Asia, it is generally expected to sing karaoke after a successful business dinner. This is the norm. And let's not forget the dancing.

You are required to literally put on your best dancing shoes in a private room with other business colleagues. Drinks and snacks are ordered, and then the singing and festivities begin. Sounds horrifying singing to a group of people, who only hours before were worthy adversaries in a business deal. Now you are joined together in a karaoke bar. It's very plausible, and likely to happen to you if it hasn't already.

If you are in Asia, my recommendation would be to not turn down the invitation when you are being asked to sing or dance after dinner. The best thing to do is prepare yourself in advance. I would recommend that you learn how to sing one or two songs in the other country's language as best as you can. Then learn one or two songs in English as a back up, in case your vocal cords give up on you from stage fright when singing your foreign song. As for the dancing, I'm sure you'll be able to call upon your earlier youthful and teenage days. But absolutely do not say no. If you do, you may cause the host to lose face in front of his staff, and that would be insulting to him. They are doing this to give themselves and you a good time, not knowing that it is causing you a sense of stress and anxiety. It is all in good faith.

This is the etiquette of the day in Asia and an expected norm. In this instance, it is karaoke, but it could be something else in another part of the world. Repeatedly, you will face diverse cultures, and you need to be flexible and open minded, within reason of course, where it will not cause physical harm to anyone.

PLAYING A GAME WITH A POTENTIAL BUSINESS CLIENT

What is in a game? There is a saying that goes like this, "discretion is the better part of valor." It was said by Falstaff in *Henry IV, Part 1*, a play by William Shakespeare. In other words: Caution is preferable to rash bravery. In business, you must decide how winning or losing will impact your potential client.

It's only a game you are playing, many would say. But the stakes are higher in business. Should you push to win or deliberately lose? By deliberately losing the game, some believe you are being deceitful. There are others that consider the deliberate act of losing to be a way to encourage the other party, lubricating the wheels of enthusiasm and diplomacy. Some would say, "Play to win at all costs." Each position has its own and varied solid defenses. You must decide if you agree with those that feel it is fine to lose (even when you can win) or those who will not allow a win unless it is deserved.

In Asia, it is always more than just a game. There's often a loss of face that comes with a defeat, and it's normal that both contestants can have a lot of face to lose. If that is the situation, then you need to think carefully before you deliberately lose the game. What are the repercussions that you may face if you win or lose? Once again, evaluate the situation and the environment you are in. The method is to ensure that the goal of the game is not downgrading anyone's character. The outcome, no matter who wins or loses, will be for the camaraderie of the game and cementing the friendship. In Asia, business is based on friendship and relations, and one needs to nurture it for the long term.

In the Western world, to deliberately lose a game is called "throwing away the game." It is not a desirable or positive expression. They are more likely to feel that by losing a game deliberately, you are in fact being deceitful. There are those that feel, by not losing, you are building the character and determination in the other person, who keeps losing and indirectly building their character.

Wherever you play, you need to assess the client's background, motivation to play, his sportsmanship, and what effect it may have on them should they lose. If your assessment is inconclusive, avoid a game until you can fully assess, then make your decision.

Even if, in your mind, it is only a game, it might not be for the other side. You may not wish to continue bludgeoning your client into defeat and submission. Showing grace with good sportsmanship, and maybe with the occasional win, is good etiquette. You make the decision though. Just remember that winning all the time does tend to get boring.

Interview Etiquette for the Job Seeker

Taking your best step forward is expected of you when you go for an interview. It begins before you step out of your door and make your way to the interview.

How you dress is an important part of how you will be perceived because, before you even open your mouth, your appearance will speak for you. Dress in clean clothes that are professional and practice good hygiene. Your shoes are a focal point too, so ensure they are clean and not soiled. If they can be polished, that is very helpful.

If you have never been to the place where you are being interviewed, then make a point of knowing it beforehand so you can arrive on time. You might even want to visit the venue beforehand so that you will be relaxed and not stressed trying to find the place on the day of the interview. It is also very possible that your interview may be online. In such a case, ensure your camera and microphone are well positioned and that there is no backlight behind your head, as this darkens your face.

Before entering the interview room or starting up the online session, make sure your phone is off and there is nothing that will disturb you. If you are meeting in person, remember the correct way to shake hands and the etiquette for that (page 123). The way you sit should be professional and no crossing of your arms. In nonverbal communication, this indicates a barrier.

Before going to my first interview, I approached a friend of mine who was a professional interviewer for new hires for his company and asked him for some advice. You will be asked many standard questions about your experience and your future intentions, so he said to be prepared for those. He also mentioned that there is a question that many people stumble on. That question is, "Why should we give you this position when there is a lineup of highly qualified applicants?" Have an impressive answer ready. Put yourself in the position of being an interviewer. They also may have many résumés, and it's possible they may misplace a few. Do not take a chance, in case the missing one is yours. Always bring extra copies to share if necessary.

Something else to keep in mind is that, if you are applying for a position at a company, you would be expected to know about the company. If asked what you know about the business, your credibility will diminish if you cannot answer. Always be prepared and do your research.

When the time has come to interact with the people interviewing you, speak calmly and clearly and take note of what they are asking you. When answering, make sure your response answers the question you were posed. When you respond, you can take a moment before answering, collecting your thoughts first. The questions are for the interviewers to assess you, so be polite, show respect, and ensure the impression you leave is a positive one. After the barrage of questions toward you has ended, there will be an opportunity for you to ask your own questions. My suggestion is to have a standard set of questions prepared in advance and to remember any questions that come to your mind during your interview. It gives the interviewers a chance to evaluate your thought process.

You may communicate verbally, but as you know, we all communicate in a non-verbal manner too, so do not overlook this aspect (page 20). Your mannerisms should be natural. Like all of your other interactions, this interview will be no different in that you apply all the rules of etiquette you have learned when dealing with people. Being polite, respectful, and courteous will come across as being very natural and sincere. You can only do your best, and if the position is for you, let fate decide.

Interview Etiquette for the Interviewer

You have been through the interview process before; you have sat in the "hot" seat. Now you are the one asking the questions. Knowing how intimidating it can be, make all the efforts you can to ensure that the interview goes smoothly and that the person being interviewed is treated with respect and professionalism.

Before meeting anyone for a business meeting or going to a dinner, you should always prepare yourself with some material in advance to learn about who you are meeting. It is no different with the interviews you are conducting. You should take time to review the people you are interviewing in advance and make notes about each person as you read their résumés.

Having been part of an interviewing panel several times, I can confirm that résumés become a blur after about the tenth résumé. Perhaps they all rank highly in terms of education and experience, but there is a missing skill you seek. Write down that missing skill and be prepared to ask about it. There might be at least one or two questions that you must have answered which will give you a more complete opinion of the applicant; have those questions ready too. Prepare all of your questions in advance when you are not influenced by external factors. This is a form of etiquette, as it displays fairness and respect to everyone.

On the day of the interview, you should be well dressed and make sure the environment where the meeting is being held is clean and comfortable with no distractions. Turn your cell phone off and ensure you are not disturbed during the interview periods.

When you meet the applicant, introduce yourself and make them feel at ease. Offer them something to drink, such as water, tea, or coffee, and have it close by. Then, once everyone is settled in, introduce the company, describe the available position, and thank them for coming in. This is no different from welcoming someone coming to your event or home and spending time with you. Let the applicant know about the entire hiring process, including what happens after the interview and subsequent follow-ups.

During the interview, you will be asking many questions. When the applicant answers, don't interrupt them and allow them to answer in their own time.

At the end of the interview, you should leave time for the applicant to ask questions of you. Encourage them to ask questions, as this opens dialogue. I have found the most valuable information is gathered during this time.

In recent times, many of the positions that are being interviewed for require the applicant to host, entertain, and meet potential clients. You might consider interviewing them in a private room in a restaurant. This creates a more realistic environment, and you can assess quickly if they possess the etiquette required to interact with clients or not.

At the end of the interview, you should be gracious and thank them for their time, as you would for a guest who leaves your home, and let them know when there will be a follow-up, if at all.

Office Party Protocols and Etiquette

The office is a sacred place. Businesses operate from offices. They are the gladiators, and the world is the arena where they trade blows with other companies hoping to win market share and translate that into profits. It is natural that there will be office parties, either in the office or outside the business premises. They can be end-of-year, Christmas, summer BBQ, or simple birthday celebrations for a colleague. The staff are the engines of this operation, and like any operation, there are rules of etiquette one must follow.

If there is an office party and one can attend, one should. If that is not possible, then at least RSVP. The normal rules of time are applicable: Arrive on time and leave on time. Although it is a more familiar setting with work colleagues, one should still be respectful. For example, it's good practice not to hover around your phone while enjoying the company of your colleagues out of the work environment.

Any party, whether office or not, is fraught with potential pitfalls. If there is alcohol served, ensure you do not drink in excess, causing yourself to be embarrassed the next day. I can recall a particular training seminar in Spain, and there was this very affable Swedish fellow who unfortunately did not manage his liquor well the first day. This behavior affected his relationship with the whole group for the entire duration of the seminar.

It is a fatal flaw to treat the office events as a place to seek romance. Some offices strictly prohibit these types of liaisons. In the revelry and in moments of weakness, human fallibility rears its head, and the consequences can be painful. Care should be exercised when speaking and talking to others, and innuendos of any kind should be restrained entirely. Despite thoughts that everyone is losing their sense of balance and measured behavior, there are those that will be watching, like your boss and other friends. Etiquette is not only for the enjoyment of times together and showing respect to those around you, but most of all it is for yourself.

One can always let one's hair down; that is what many do at parties. However, this is different because tomorrow you will come back and face these people, and your good or bad behavior will remain etched in their memories. If you see a colleague getting into a potentially difficult situation with questionable actions that will have negative repercussions, take them aside perhaps and assist if at all possible. Office parties are welcomed, but caution needs to be exercised and so must etiquette.

When to Reciprocate Buying a Drink

The fame of the English, Irish, and Scottish pubs have crossed the seas to continents across the world. Think of the famous limericks, sayings, and quotes we use today; many found their birth in pubs and bars among those nations. One of them is the common expression "It's my round" or "It's my shout." If you have been invited for a round of drinks, should you always reciprocate? Before answering this question, let's think about what those expressions mean. When someone shouts out one of those phrases, it means they will be responsible for buying their group the next round of drinks. If you have had the generosity of others during the evening and have yet to reciprocate by buying the others a drink, should you? The simple answer is absolutely. Not to do so would be poor etiquette, especially if you are in the United Kingdom.

It does not really matter which country you are in or what phrase you might use; it's considered good etiquette that, if you were bought several rounds of drinks by others or have been invited several times for dinners, you should reciprocate at least occasionally. It is the right and proper thing to do.

Sometimes someone, in a moment of madness, will say, "Everything's on me tonight." Those are saved for occasions when you get a hole in one at golf. It is etiquette that, if you do mange to snag a hole in one at golf, you should buy everyone present at the clubhouse a drink. Given that it can be a very burdensome bill, many clubs have taken out a hole-in-one insurance for such events. Personally, after the initial excitement and at a later occasion, if I meet the holder of a hole-in-one event, I buy them a drink. Although there is no obligation, it's always a lovely gesture if you are able to do so.

In Asia, it is quite common to see different parties within a dinner group having a fight at the restaurant to see who has the privilege of paying the bill for the entire group. It is a standard ritual to see who is off their blocks the quickest to capture the server and pay the bill. It all is really a matter of face, signifying "I respect you all so much, so allow me to pay for the meal." When you see rowdy scenes like this, next time you know what it is all about. In this instance, if you have the chance to reciprocate, do so. To ensure that you succeed in paying first next time, make an arrangement with the owner of the restaurant in advance to take your payment only.

Etiquette is to show respect, politeness, and grace to yourself and others around you. What better way than sharing that with good friends in the form of buying them a drink or even a meal. It certainly is good etiquette and not something to shy away from. Do such things with the greatest of intentions and expecting the least back in return. The greatest gift in life, apart from life itself, is to have friends. If you have friends to whom you can reciprocate their kindness, you are blessed.

Private Business Club Etiquette

Private clubs are very much alive and active in many parts of the world. There is a private club reciprocity program that, if you belong to a private club in your own city and that club has associate club reciprocity, then you can visit those clubs located in other countries and cities. Without this reciprocity you cannot enter them. These types of clubs are not open to the public.

There is certain protocol that you should be aware of when you are invited to such clubs. Generally, the member of the club who has invited you should greet you at the reception area and escort you to where you are going to have a meeting or a meal. If they are unable to greet you at the reception, the host should inform reception they have a guest arriving and the staff will escort the guest to where the host is. When you arrive at the reception and you do not see your host, let the personnel at reception know you are expected, and they can find the host or take previous instructions to escort you. No attempt should be made to seek out your host on your own.

One of the hated and frowned upon modern-day actions is to speak on your cell phone in public areas. At a private club, it is the one sanctuary where cell phones are not to be used openly. Furthermore, you are expected to turn your phone off or set it on silent without vibration. Clubs previously did not encourage phone usage at all during your visit to the club. All clubs have different policies, and those that do not allow calls have a separate area where you can go to receive and make calls if you must. This is the only area where you can use your phone. Be sure to know the rules of the club you are visiting.

There is also a dress code. If not adhered to, you will not be permitted. When visiting the Oxford and Cambridge Club in London, they have a specific dress code, and The American Hong Kong Club in Hong Kong is equally strict. I do not recommend testing the code, so stay away from torn clothing or jeans and opt for business casual. It may save you the time of having to go back and change.

Should you be invited for a meal at the club, you will not be required to pay. The club will not accept payment from visitors, only club members. The bill will be dealt with even more discreetly than at a standard restaurant. The club will not expect you to pay, nor should you offer to do so in front of the server, as this might embarrass your host. If you wish to reciprocate, then invite the member out on another occasion.

It is inevitable that your host will introduce you to certain colleagues that he bumps into at the club. If any one of these new introductions has an interest in sharing personal contact information with you, I would suggest you reply by asking them to please connect with the host, and they will be happy to pass on that information. That is more for courtesy. If the host encourages exchanges of contact details at the time of the meeting, then feel free to do so.

Apart from the discreet nature of these clubs, the ambience is very rewarding, and the correct use and knowledge of appropriate etiquette is appreciated.

CONCLUSION

BEING A GENTLEMAN CANNOT BE DEFINED OR CLASSIFIED as knowing how to open doors for ladies, hold a glass of Cognac, match a whiskey and cigar, decant a bottle of wine, and eat correctly with a fork and knife. No, no, no, no, that is far too simplistic.

Equally, neither can a lady be simply defined or classified by what she wears, the perfume she favors, or the way she walks, talks, and socializes. Nay, that is far too artless and disingenuous.

When we are well armed with knowledge, both formal and informal, we should put this knowledge to practical use in our daily lives. No matter what we, as gentlemen and ladies, face on the different highways of life and different cultural roads we tread, we must do so with a bursting optimism in our heart, indefatigable endurance, and an unflappable faith in ourselves.

Today's modern ladies and gentlemen are fully aware that we live in a fast-paced, changing world. A world where cultural identities are no longer cordoned off by geography. Instead, we have a multitude of different cultures living side by side in a multitude of cities all across the globe. This is the norm, not the exception.

The well-mannered and etiquette-conscious citizen of today must know a myriad of skills, including how to eat with hands, chopsticks, knives and forks. Yes indeed, but they also need to eat humility, lies, and untruths, then digest it all, filtering it through an internal gauze comprised of sound principles like honesty, fairness, and loyalty. The residue is discarded, and the remains are sifted, refined, and molded into a material extracting qualities of balanced and measured judgement, vital to developing the skeletal framework of a modern gentleman. Time, circumstances, and change have demanded that this mold be forged with a stern and uncompromising material, for today's tumultuous world requires it.

Today's world demands that we all must learn, appreciate, and understand all cultures, not just national cultures, but cultures of faith, the culture of oneself, and generational cultures. Then, and only then, can an outline and character of a true gentleman and refined lady arise. There is more yet. Their rough, untested frames must still be thrust through the burning flames that will sear at their core values to craft true, well-mannered people of the world who are understanding, compassionate, polite and respectful, fair and gracious to all. Only then will everything fall into place.

To be a modern-day lady or gentleman, abide by the points of the enlightening compass.

Learn about yourself. Understand what is your right and wrong and question it, deeply, soulfully, and recalibrate it to accommodate all that you have learned after your introspection.

Understand other people's culture through their language, food, music, arts, and history. Don't criticize, don't blame or feel pity for them, but understand and respect them.

Some things you must learn, and some things you know inside your heart are the right thing to do. Some things, the wrong things, you must walk away from. Have the strength to do it.

Hone your skills to being a better person day by day, minute by minute, and second by second, and then start the cycle over again and again and again.

Once you have captured and mastered the intricacies of these points to become intertwined within yourself as a daily habit, then, and only then, will you have in the palms of your hand and in the depths of your heart the compassion of understanding others in a respectful and dignified manner. You will be a master of the art of etiquette and manners.

ACKNOWLEDGMENTS

THE PHYSICAL ACT OF WRITING A BOOK is minute when compared to a lifetime of experiences. Writing this book was unexpectedly one of the most gratifying adventures I have had. You experience heights of vibrancy, moments of contemplation, and pure joy as you recall experiences kept in the deep crevices of your mind. I became reacquainted with myself during this writing journey, and at the end of it all, I can describe it as a wonderfully cathartic experience for me.

When writing a book of this nature, the author alone is one tune in the melody. You need the strength and power of an orchestra to make it alive. It requires exceptional teamwork. My orchestra and team were matchless, faultless, and superbly professional. I would like to thank Page Street Publishing and my editor Marissa Giambelluca for having faith and reaching out to me, as well as the book cover designer and all the other production-related support team members and Macmillan for making this book into a reality.

Enormous thanks to my followers on social media for their support. Their many questions and comments over the years were a major factor in my decision to write this book.

A special thanks to Carmen Lee, my colleague and friend of many years, for making this avenue of my life open into a new world for me, where my life experience can reach out to countless others. Your gentle but forceful and continual words of encouragement were reassuring, especially when writing on cold mornings was the last thing on my mind. Your unspoken words of "You can do it" echoed with each character typed on my keyboard.

Deep thanks to my lifelong friend, from whom I learned so much about life, Professor Victor Levine. Recalling our experiences in life and sharing memorable times together with you has enriched me.

To all the wonderful people who touched my life either in a work or travel capacity, your experience is mine as well. Close friends, acquaintances, associates, and countless nameless strangers, I thank you. Whether we were sharing experiences while waiting at a sunless train lounge, on the choppy waters of the sea when cruising, bathing on the shores of the Mediterranean, exchanging stories at 32,000 feet in the air sitting next to one another for ten hours on a plane, enjoying the thrill of the casino in Monte Carlo, or drinking a cup of cappuccino at a café, each of those moments was very meaningful to me and I am grateful.

Wherever we may have met—the plateaus of Ethiopia, the Pampas of Argentina, the Americas, South to North and across Africa, the coast, and the vineyards of China—thank you all for sharing your special life experiences with me and giving me a life filled with rich moments that have made me a better person. Thank you.

ABOUT THE AUTHOR

DR. CLINTON LEE is an internationally recognized intercultural etiquette expert, as well as a wine and spirit educator and judge. He is the founder of the Asia Pacific Wine and Spirit Institute and uses his expertise in the management of his vineyard in British Columbia, Canada. His work and travels have taken him to five continents and over one hundred countries. He has lectured at Simon Fraser University in Canada. Dr. Lee has over twenty years of experience providing consultancy and training in Canada, China, Singapore, Hong Kong, Argentina, France, Hungary, Portugal, Italy, and the United States. Dr. Lee has been featured internationally in the media and is recognized as a social media influencer with over two million followers on several platforms and has had over one billion views on his video content. He consults across Europe, Asia, and North America. Dr. Lee is a popular and sought-after influencer and interviewer.

Connect with him at www.apwasi.com, or follow him (apwasiwine) on Instagram, TikTok, and YouTube.

INDEX